Joshua Schwimmer

EUNY HONG is a journalist and author with international experience in web, print, and television
news. Her work has appeared in *The New York
Times*, *The Washington Post*, *The Wall Street Journal
Europe*, *International Herald Tribune*, *The New Republic*, *The Boston Globe*, and *Forward*. She was previously a columnist at the *Financial Times* and a
web producer at France 24 in Paris. She is the
author of one previous book, the novel *Kept: A
Comedy of Sex and Manners*. She is fluent in English,
French, German, and Korean. She holds a BA in
philosophy from Yale University and is a former
Fulbright Scholar.

## ALSO BY EUNY HONG

*Kept: A Comedy of Sex and Manners*

# THE
# BIRTH
···· OF ····
# KOREAN
# COOL

# THE
# BIRTH
## OF
# KOREAN
# COOL

## HOW ONE NATION IS
## CONQUERING THE WORLD
## THROUGH POP CULTURE

# EUNY HONG

PICADOR

NEW YORK

The names and identifying characteristics of some persons described in this book have been changed, as have dates, places, and other details of events depicted in the book.

www.picadorusa.com
www.twitter.com/picadorusa • www.facebook.com/picadorusa
picadorbookroom.tumblr.com

For book club information, please visit www.facebook.com/picadorbookclub or e-mail marketing@picadorusa.com.

*Designed by Steven Seighman*

Library of Congress Cataloging-in-Publication Data

Hong, Euny.
    The birth of Korean cool : how one nation is conquering the world through pop culture / Euny Hong.
        p. cm.
    ISBN 978-1-250-04511-9 (trade paperback)
    ISBN 978-1-250-04512-6 (e-book)
    1. Korea (South)—Social life and customs.   2. Popular culture—Korea (South).   3. Hong, Euny.   I. Title.
    DS923.23.H66 2014
    306.095195—dc23
                                                        2014012175

Picador books may be purchased for educational, business, or promotional use. For information on bulk purchases, please contact Macmillan Corporate and Premium Sales Department at 1-800-221-7945, extension 5442, or write specialmarkets@macmillan.com.

First Edition: August 2014

10  9  8  7  6  5  4  3  2

*To my childhood nanny, Mrs. Terebush, who gave me a love of reading, without which I could not have become a writer.*

# AUTHOR'S NOTE

. . . . . . . . . . . . . . . .

"Korea" refers to South Korea, unless otherwise specified. Names of Korean individuals will appear using the Korean convention, last name followed by given name, unless the person has opted to use the Western name convention.

# CONTENTS

• • • • • • • • • • •

Character is destiny.

Heraclitus (c. 535–c. 475 BC)

# THE
# BIRTH
## OF
# KOREAN
# COOL

# INTRODUCTION

. . . . . . . . . . . . . . . .

KOREA WAS NOT COOL IN 1985.

That was the year that my parents decided, after spending nearly twenty years in the United States, to move back to Seoul, South Korea—specifically, to Gangnam, the wealthy neighborhood whose famed "style" was to be the subject of rapper Psy's song.

I was twelve years old; my sisters were nine and seven, respectively. At the time, I strongly favored the move. My early childhood in the Chicago suburb where we lived was full of corn, beef, milk, hay fever, and racists. It's implausible, but sadly true, that eight-year-old boys would call me "Jap," as if they were Marines during World War II checking trees for snipers. I would just put up with it; why explain that I was actually Korean, when in those days Korea was still linked to an unpopular war in which many American soldiers were killed? Whenever kids asked me, "Are you Chinese?"—which was often—I would invariably respond yes. My mother heard me doing this once and gave me hell for it. "Why didn't you say you were Korean?" she asked. I was not doing that again, not after an incident in first grade in which a boy told me: "You're lying. There is no such place." I remember briefly wondering whether my parents had been bullshitting me about where they came from.

I was eager to leave this life and embrace the new one: Korea was my Zion. I had read too many British novels about wretched children finding out they were actually of noble birth and I was expecting to be salaamed upon arriving at the Seoul airport.

Now, yes, South Korea is rich and increasingly futuristic. It's easy to forget that in 1965, South Korea's per capita GDP was less than that of Ghana, and even less than that of North Korea. As recently as the 1970s, North and South Korea's GDP were neck and neck.

Today, South Korea is the world's fifteenth largest economy and Seoul resembles the type of space-age city that Arthur C. Clarke imagined in his novel *2001: A Space Odyssey*. Plans are underway to construct an "invisible" skyscraper near Seoul—one that will use cameras and LEDs to create the illusion from a distance that the building is not there. Every single subway car has two wi-fi hotspots so that people can watch their morning TV shows on their Samsung Galaxy phones—benefiting from a superfast Internet connection that never gets interrupted even when the subway is going through tunnels or below water. Korea is widely considered one of the greatest economic miracles of the modern day.

What most of the world doesn't know—or has forgotten—is the painful period between poverty and wealth. Within a matter of decades, South Korea went through changes that most wealthy nations took hundreds of years to achieve: social changes as radical as those brought about by the French Revolution and economic changes as radical as those brought on by the Industrial Revolution.

Bridges, skyscrapers, and highways appeared seemingly out of nowhere; it was almost like watching a time-lapse video. Meanwhile, everyone was clamoring for their rights: women, students, the newly rich, the old aristocracy, laborers, white-collar workers. It was a cacophonous and chaotic time to live in Seoul, but it was also an amazing time. Few people can boast, as I can, that they saw Rome being built in a day.

Other countries have gone from rags to riches in the last century, but among these, only South Korea has the cheek to set its sights on becoming the world's top exporter of popular culture.

South Korean soap operas, music, movies, video games, and junk food already dominate the Asian cultural scene. In fact, South Korea has been the tastemaker of Asia for over a decade, and its westward expansion is inevitable. You may not even realize that it is already underway.

You may have an iPhone, for example, but its microchips are made by Apple's biggest competitor—the Korean electronics company Samsung.

The Korean wave of popular culture is called "Hallyu." You should learn the word, since you'll be seeing a lot of it. U.S. President Barack Obama referred to it during a March 2012 visit to South Korea, in the context of discussing the nation's technical and pop culture innovations. He said: "It's no wonder so many people around the world have caught the Korean Wave—Hallyu."

It would not be an exaggeration to say that Hallyu is the world's biggest, fastest cultural paradigm shift in modern history.

How did Korea sneak up from behind?

Well, in 1994, when the United States and the United Kingdom were kicking and screaming in protest against converting from analog to digital TV—some people even arguing that "this fascist government can't force me to buy a new TV"—Korea was busy wiring the entire country for Internet broadband with government funds, just like building a national highway or railway system. This new mode of transport would be everything that Korea wasn't: uninhibited, multilingual, indifferent to class and hierarchy, not boxed in by ocean on three sides and an aggressive totalitarian state on the fourth side, and ready to risk being barraged by uncensored and possibly seditious material. Openness was not an inherently Korean trait: nineteenth-century explorers from the West dubbed it the Hermit Kingdom. But what enticed the nation was not so much the virtual cargo that these new channels would bring in; it was what Korea was planning to send out to the world that really mattered.

Did South Koreans know that "Gangnam Style" would be the song that put K-pop on the map? Of course not. But they knew it would happen eventually. They had been setting up the mechanism for pop culture domination since the dawn of the World Wide Web in the 1990s.

One might well ask, why focus on pop culture when this area has been the near-exclusive domain of the United States for a century? Because South Korea is developing its soft power.

"Soft power," a term coined in 1990 by Harvard political scientist Joseph Nye, is the intangible power a country wields through its image rather than through force. Hard power is military might or economic coercion. Soft power, on the other hand, is how the United States got the world to buy its Marlboro Reds and Levi's jeans: by peddling a desirable image. By peddling cool.

It wasn't the United States' tank technology or its impressive show of muscle in invading Grenada that made the kids in communist Yugoslavia want to pay two months' wages for black market Levi's 501 jeans. It was James Dean.

Now, Korea wants to have this kind of cultural cachet—even in the West—but it's not relying on "Gangnam Style" and K-pop. I don't think that Koreans, if they're being honest with themselves, believe their music will take up significant market share in the United States or western Europe. Instead, it's about getting the crucial but still dormant third-world market hooked on Korean pop culture—eastern Europe, the Arab nations, and soon, Africa. The addiction has already begun; in Iran, the Korean historical costume drama *The Jewel in the Palace* is so popular that Iranians have reportedly begun organizing their mealtimes so as not to interfere with the show's broadcast time.

Right now, the third-world countries are too poor for most western nations to care about. This is where Korea has a peculiar, unreproducible advantage over every single other nation that has been a global pop culture power: it was once a third-world country. Thus Korea understands the stages of other nations' development; it has carefully studied these cultures to determine what kinds of "K-culture" products would be most favored there. And Korean economists are hard at work gauging the rate at which these nations will become wealthier and have more purchasing power. You can bet that once the citizens of these countries are able to afford to buy mobile phones and washing machines, they'll buy Korean brands. Why? They're already hooked on Korea the Brand.

If this sounds like a national campaign, that's because it is. The South Korean government has made the Korean Wave the nation's number one priority.

Korea has multiple five-year plans, the likes of which most democratic and capitalist countries have never seen. The government felt that spreading Korean culture worldwide was dependent on Internet ubiquity, so they subsidized Internet access for the poor, the elderly, and the disabled. Currently, the government is wiring every single household with a 1 gigabit-per-second connection—which would make it two hundred times faster than the average Internet connection in the United States. South Korea learned from having to rebuild its country after the Korean War (1950–1953) that if you're going to make change, the change has to be drastic, it has to be fast, and it has to be for everyone. E-mail is useless if only a few people have it.

And it's not just the government who has five-year plans; private Korean enterprises have them too. A Korean record label will spend five to seven years grooming a future K-pop star. This is why some Korean artists sign the thirteen-year contracts binding them to indentured servitude; the first half of that period is spent on training, and the company can't reap the rewards of its investment unless the artist stays on past the incubation period.

The South Korean economy is a paradox: it is utterly capitalist, yet at the same time it is in some ways still a command economy. From the earliest days of its independence from Japanese rule following World War II, the South Korean government has intervened in private industry.

In addition to building a high-tech Internet infrastructure, South Korea is one of only a handful of countries whose government pours its own money into investing in its nation's start-ups. In 2012, government funds constituted over 25 percent of all venture capital money disbursed in Korea.[1] A mind-boggling one-third of venture capital in Korea is spent on the entertainment industry—more than on any other sector.

And here's another five-year plan: in 2009, when the South Korean record industry was suffering a loss in revenue because of illegal music downloads, the government allocated $91 million to rescue K-pop. The plan included building a K-pop center with a three-thousand-seat concert hall (a work in progress) and regulating the nation's *noraebangs*—karaoke rooms—to make sure the owners are paying royalties for all the songs in their machines. Most countries would never stand for using public funds to audit karaoke rooms.

It's an idea so ridiculous that only South Korea would think of it.

The nation has decided that the twenty-first century will be Korea's century, just as the twentieth century was America's century. And it's not enough for Korea to make semiconductors and cars; it has to be cool as well. Of course, Korea is upending the widely held belief that trying too hard to be cool makes you uncool.

Perhaps the person who best expressed Korea's fearlessness, ambition, and never-ending gall was Korean music mogul Jin-young Park (head of the record label JYP.) When asked by western music executives, "Where are you from?" he would reply cryptically, "I am from the future."[2]

Welcome to Korea. Welcome to the future.

# 1

# BEFORE COOL

• • • • • • • • • • • • • • • •

WHEN MY FAMILY MOVED TO KOREA, IN 1985, IT WAS still a developing country. The only mitigating factor was that we would be living not just in Gangnam but in the Apgujeong neighborhood—the most elite district—and in the Hyundai Apartments—the most elite residence. For us, it was rent-free, thrown in as part of my father's hiring package. He was the beneficiary of a desperate plan by the Korean government to reverse the brain drain it suffered from the 1950s onward, following the Korean War. In those days, anyone with any gumption fled to the United States for graduate school. Somewhat stupidly, the Korean government made sure that only the best and brightest of its students were granted exit visas. My parents and anyone else seeking to get their PhD in the United States had to sit for a difficult exam; if you failed, you couldn't leave the country, regardless of whether the U.S. embassy granted you permission to enter the United States.

For some reason, Korea's leaders were certain that people

like my parents would want to return to the rubbly, corrupt mess that was Korea after getting their U.S. degrees; they didn't anticipate just how many of those students would make the United States their home.

Thus in the 1970s and 1980s, the Korean government lured people like my father—an economist—back to Korea with the promise of titles, carte blanche to run their own research institutes or labs, free apartments, servants, and chauffeurs.

For the most part, however, my family's transition to South Korea didn't go quite as expected. We did get the maid, as promised, but she had never seen a vacuum cleaner before and was so afraid of the noise she refused to use ours. Obviously, the South Korea that was master of cutting-edge technology had not yet come into being. The Hyundai Apartments were the poshest in the city, but they comprised hundreds of identical beige buildings. The view out our window was monotonous; it looked like something from the Eastern Bloc. The elevator was frequently out of order and sometimes I had to walk up to our apartment on the tenth floor. Brownouts and water shutoffs were common occurrences.

Korean technology was famously terrible in those days. The fact that the world has forgotten this is a testament to how successful Korea's national branding strategy has been. Among the expat community, the Korean electronics company Samsung used to be referred to as Samsuck. I would stand at a huge distance when using one of its microwave ovens because I was afraid they were leaking radiation.

Moving from the United States to the third world meant being stripped of many comforts; on the other hand, only by moving from an American suburb to a poor, grimy city could I ever have appreciated the excitement of being a pretend street urchin.

My mother had forbidden my sisters and me to eat street food, but we did it anyway: roasted chestnuts and sweet potatoes, always cooked over a large tin with holes punctured in the lid and a piece of coal inside. Even now, the smell of burnt sugar makes me think of *bobki* biscuits, made from a mixture of caramelized sugar and baking soda, sold on the street by old ladies with short, tightly permed hair.

I wouldn't describe the biscuits as tasty; cooked baking soda is bitter and its astringent properties make your mouth pucker. But I think the sensory shock was half the enjoyment; the other half was watching it being made: It was like watching a blacksmith make bullets, or a dealer prepare heroin. The women would melt the white powdery mixture in a metal ladle held over a huge piece of burning coal. When the powder melted it would froth quickly and turn brown. This would be poured into a flat, circular mold with some sort of imprinted design in the middle—a bird or a star. Once the mixture hardened, we'd take the paper-thin wafer straight from the mold and eat it while it was still hot. For some reason, it was really important to maintain the integrity of the design embossed in the middle of the biscuit; if it broke, there would be audible moans of disappointment. In recent years, these biscuit women have all but disappeared.

Seoul had supermarkets of course, but in those days, the street food merchants played a much more prominent role, scattered chaotically on the sidewalks all over the city. I loved it; I felt as if I were living in a medieval city, or at least what I imagined a medieval city would look like, based on Monty Python sketches. (Especially Pythonesque were Seoul's many roasted silkworm larvae stands; I could never get my head around those.)

Every summer, a woman would put up a trampoline in an abandoned lot near my house, and for 200 won (around 15 cents), one could jump on it for half an hour. Standing by the trampoline was what she did all day; sole proprietor, sole employee.

These kinds of mini-enterprises, like the trampoline, prolonged the precious, Elysian period of childhood in a way that I did not see in the United States, where kids started hanging out at the mall and acted like teenyboppers from age nine or ten.

Childhood friendships in Korea were devoted and physical; it was common for same-sex platonic friends to walk the street holding hands or with their arms around each other's waists. My friends were astonished that it was not like that everywhere. In the sixth grade, a classmate asked me, "Is it true that in America, people call you a 'homo' if you hold hands with your friends?" I had to say yes.

I have not witnessed this kind of physicality among friends except maybe in the Arab world. As South Korea got richer, I saw a decline in same-sex hand-holding among children. I don't have a good explanation except for some platitudes about how wealth destroys intimacy. Or kids just got too cool to be so demonstrative.

My real Proustian madeleine, though, is mothballs.

The odor of mothballs always make me think of Seoul's toilets, because when I arrived in Seoul, mothballs were hung in public bathrooms as a deodorizer. Nowadays, many Seoul toilets are electronic and have self-cleaning features as well as nozzles that squirt water and rinse and blow-dry. Individual stalls also sometimes have buttons you can press to play light music so people don't have to hear how you've chosen to spend your time in the stall. Those toilet bowls are cleaner than the tables of some restaurants. But back in 1985, oh my god.

First-worlders have the luxury of not having to think about waste elimination very much. But for a third-worlder, poop is a big preoccupation. To the average American, a toilet is a place to enter and exit without being traumatized; there are extractor fans to erase odors; toilets flush all evidence of one's activities, and blue bleach tablets kept in the septic tank save users from having to see the real color of their pee in the bowl. There is soap and hot water and hand dryers or paper towels so that one can emerge even cleaner than when one entered. A toilet should be like a waiter at a good restaurant: if it's doing its job properly, one shouldn't notice it's there.

So imagine my surprise upon arriving in Seoul to discover that the majority of the toilets were the squatting kind, where you had to stand with your legs spread wide, and void over a basin in the floor with no water in it. It was not always flushable.

Then there was the annual school poop collection.

As in many developing nations, some of the basic health

procedures in South Korea were handled at the public schools. We all got our inoculations from the school nurse, for example. We'd line up in order of student number, which was determined at the beginning of the year by height. The nurse used the same needle for all the students, disinfecting between each injection by running the needle through the flame of a candle.

Along the same lines, schoolwide tests for intestinal parasites were conducted too. The teacher would distribute white envelopes the size of a credit card. Then the teacher would remind us, "Please write your name on the envelope *before* you put your poop in, because you'll find it difficult to write on it afterward."

The next day at school, the samples would be collected in a big bag. Invariably, some students would not have their sample, and the teacher would hit them on the head or the arm. The students would always say as they were getting thwacked, "But I didn't poop yesterday, teacher!" and then everyone would laugh.

Supposedly the samples were sent to some national lab to be inspected for parasites; the lab would then send deworming pills to the affected students. I don't think my school had any cases of parasites during my time there; at that point, parasites were ceasing to become a serious problem. While far from ideal, South Korea's health conditions by 1985 were far better than they had been just a few years prior.

It might seem somewhat tyrannical to make millions of schoolchildren defecate on command, but it's obvious that disease eradication works only if everyone gets treatment—not just a select few volunteers. Perhaps as a result of these methods, Korea has rid itself of parasites and nearly every other health problem that plagues underdeveloped nations.[1]

My middle school happened to be the testing ground for a number of educational experiments in those days, so it was a good vantage point from which to witness the rapid changes in Korea. We were among the first schools to ban school uniforms, which were seen as an imprisoning holdover from the period of Japanese colonial rule, which lasted from 1910 to 1945. In practice, though, the liberal dress code had so many restrictions that they might as well have reinstated the uniform. We weren't allowed to wear clothes with any non-Korean lettering on them. We also weren't allowed to perm our hair (although in retrospect, they were just trying to save us from ourselves). If you had naturally wavy hair, you literally had to have a doctor's note to prove it.

Even North Korea exercised less hair totalitarianism. According to some leaked North Korean barbershop posters, the late Kim Jong-il permitted perms as one of the eighteen accepted hairstyles for women. (Based on photos of North Korean government officials, the perm seems to be almost mandatory for men.)

My school was one of the early adopters of co-education post-elementary school. Most kids I knew in Seoul thought I was lucky to be in a co-ed school. I didn't.

For one thing, girls had to take home economics and boys took engineering. I loved home ec, but we did learn some pretty weird lessons. My eighth-grade home ec teacher told us, "If you want to start out right with a marriage, always cook the food your husband likes, not the food you like. Your children will naturally develop the same tastes as your husband."

Gender was still an indicator of destiny. Starting from tenth grade, South Korean students had to study another foreign language in addition to English. Excellent idea. But at many high schools, they would only let boys take German and girls take French. No boys allowed in French class and no girls allowed in German class. No exceptions.

But Korea has made giant strides in leveling the playing field for women. Until as recently as 1991, South Korean women were not permitted to be the head of the household, meaning they could not make legal decisions on behalf of the family. In the event of a divorce, a wife was not entitled to an equal division of property and children were automatically granted to the father's custody.

Just two decades later, in December 2012, South Korea elected its first female president, Park Geun-hye.

How does a national mind-set alter so drastically within the space of three decades? It's not just that Korea became wealthy; oil-rich Arab nations are swimming in money, but they haven't advanced much socially. In some instances, they've regressed, thanks to the resurgence of Islamic fundamentalism. China is becoming frighteningly influential on the global finance scene, but its vastness, huge population, and warring ethnic factions make it difficult for the government to effect rapid, centralized nationwide changes. Part of

Korea's plan all along was to achieve what many other newly rich nations couldn't—to transform the country from the inside out; socially, culturally, and mentally. Has it worked? Well, something's different all right. For one thing, the emergence of irony.

# 2

# THE BIRTH OF IRONY

. . . . . . . . . . . . . . . .

## WHAT IS IRONY AND HOW CAN YOU GET IT?

Irony is that special privilege of wealthy nations; the best purveyors of irony live at the very height of their society's prosperity and influence, which allows them the leisure (if not the freedom) to wax philosophic and write. Besides, it is in times of success that decadence, bluster, hypocrisy, and all the other favored topics for satire are at a fever pitch. Aristophanes, possibly the world's first satirist, wrote his plays as Athens was becoming the dominant power in the region. Cervantes wrote at the height of Spain's naval wealth. And Alexander Pope was born the year that England defeated the Spanish Armada. First, one scrambles for wealth; then one luxuriates in mocking the effeteness that comes with it.

"Gangnam Style" and its 2013 follow-up song "Gentlemen" signaled the emergence of irony in South Korea, marking the country's final stage in its modern evolution. If you don't think that irony is a measure of an elite society, think of how annoyed you were the last time you were accused of not having any. Americans have told me that Asians have no irony; in Europe, where I lived recently, I was told that Americans have none.

South Korea had no irony when I arrived. I can say that as honestly as I can say that it had no McDonald's (it arrived in 1988, in Gangnam, of course). The Korean language has no word for irony, nor for parody, which is why the Korean press has been using the English word "parody" to describe "Gangnam Style."

"Gangnam Style," the song and the video, are full of inside jokes about South Korea's nouveaux riches. For example, in the opening shot, Psy appears to be lounging on a beach; when the camera pulls away, it's revealed he's in an unattractive urban playground. Psy boasts of his tough-guy prowess, singing that he can down a coffee in one gulp, as if he were talking about downing a shot of 100 proof alcohol. This is Psy's way of saying, you Gangnam types may be rich and fancy, but your roots are humble, you've become a bunch of wusses with too many skin products, and what's more, this city still needs cleaning up.

During the period that I lived in South Korea—the late 1980s and early 1990s—there was a steep climb in the nation's economic development. I witnessed Seoul's transformation from a grim, dangerously crowded place where all designer clothes were counterfeit to a glamorous, rich global megacity where—as Psy's "Gangnam Style" video shows—people are fabulously well dressed but still hang out in parking garages because Seoul is overcrowded and there isn't enough open space.

I attended Gu-jung elementary and middle school—the highest-rated, most entitled, most hated school in the entire country. Because of our school and our neighborhood's privileged status, we students were expected to act in a manner befitting that reputation. My friend, who also grew up in Apgujeong, had a little brother who ended up going to high school north of the Han River (*gangnam* means "south of the river"). When his classmates found out he was from Apgujeong, they called him *bujajip*—rich kid—and beat him bloody every day. He started ditching class and eventually transferred to an international school.

In 1987, every schoolchild in South Korea made a mandatory donation toward the construction of the Peace Dam, a project of then-president Chun Doo-hwan. The North Koreans were allegedly building a dam of mass destruction close to the north-south border; it would collect water flowing from the north and then one day, when we least expected it, North Korea would unleash the water and flatten Seoul. The retaliatory Peace Dam, to be built in the south, would send the water back north. I do not pretend to understand the engineering involved.

We had all brought the recommended donation of 200 won. The teacher hit all of us that day, one at a time, with her wooden stick wrapped with black electrical tape.

"You are from Gangnam," the teacher said, a phrase she used often, as if she were intoning, "This is Sparta." "If the nationwide minimum is 200 won, you have to bring at least 1,000 won. You shouldn't have to be told."

You can't be ironic when you're being hit with a stick

wrapped with black electrical tape. Or, when you're being forced to prepare a speech every semester to enter in your school's Anti-Communist Speech Contest.

South Korea wanted nothing more than for its GDP to skyrocket, but it was dismayed with the widening gap between the classes. Since I lived in the wealthiest neighborhood, I was at the epicenter of competing ideals for the nation. Gangnam was a nutty place to live in the 1980s and 1990s.

My school enforced rules to make the increasing income disparities less visible. Students were not permitted to wear watches exceeding 20,000 won in value or shoes that cost more than 9,000 won—about $15 and $7, respectively. We were not permitted to be picked up or dropped off at school by private car; this became a matter of controversy, since students were often required to stay at school very late into the night, so safety was a concern.

Korean law prohibited private tutors for school subjects, for fear that this would give an advantage to the wealthy (this law has since been repealed). Most students at my school had them anyway. Periodically, the school would give the students a sort of denunciation pop quiz, with questions such as "Who among your classmates is receiving private tutoring?"

My family was not Gangnam-rich. Definitely not Psy-rich. And not as rich as one of my high school classmates who, in the summer of 1989, flew with her little brother to Hawaii for just one weekend because her brother wanted to see the movie *Batman* (the Michael Keaton version) on opening night and he couldn't wait for the film to come to Korea.

Nor were we as rich as the girl who misplaced a $20,000 violin and did not even bother to look for it because her parents would buy a new one.

Nonetheless, my father had a chauffeur. It was a professional necessity. Any Korean executive showing up to a lunch meeting in a car he drove himself would be laughed out of the restaurant.

The acquisition of wealth is not funny. It was especially unfunny for the titled aristocracy in South Korea who were watching the earth start to crack beneath them. For people like—may I be frank?—my family. We did not sit around making dry, witty existential comments as these vulgar nouveaux riches rose up among us and started showing up at the fish market in mink coats.

It was a life ripe for irony, but irony did not arrive until much later, after I had already given up on Korea and had no desire to return.


Psy (né Park Jae-sang) was definitely not the conquering hero Korea wanted to lead its shock-and-awe cultural invasion. Korea had been priming more conventional, beautiful K-pop bands, like the nine-member girl group Girls' Generation, who were already deified superstars in Asia. But those groups never really gained significant appeal in the west.

Koreans were not expecting that the man to bring Hallyu to the western stage would be the class clown of the Korean music world, a man who intentionally showed off his sweaty, hairy armpits and potato-shaped body, who made fart jokes in his songs, and whose outfits looked as though they were picked out by a Las Vegas stage magician.

Psy is the paradigm shift within the paradigm shift. And his life and bewildering rise to fame are an embodiment of the changes in Korea and Korean society over the last few decades.

Psy and I share a few things in common. We both grew up in Gangnam, Seoul's wealthiest and slickest district. We both come from "good" and studious families. Our dads went to the same high school; our moms attended the same university. However, I was born in the United States and only lived in Gangnam during junior high and high school, whereas Psy was born and raised there. Every cell in his body was nurtured by Gangnam air and water. His family are tycoons going back a few generations; they are among the oldest of the Gangnam new money. His father, Park Won-ho, is chairman of the Korean semiconductor company DI Corp. Psy was born with a real Gangnam silver spoon in his mouth.

The western press frequently mentions that Psy studied at Boston University and the Berklee College of Music (though it is unclear whether he got a degree), but has very little information about his childhood, which is surprising given that Psy has the most-viewed YouTube video of all time.

Meanwhile, the Korean media has extensive information on Psy. So why hasn't any of this made its way into the western press? Because Korean media coverage of Psy's childhood makes no sense outside the Korean cultural context. Korean media has focused on his notoriously bad relationship with his parents—particularly his father—which he has mentioned in many interviews. It's clear he's deeply ashamed of it: in Korea, where the Confucian belief that all virtue stems from filial piety holds sway, not getting along with one's parents is quite a big deal. But in the western media, the press wouldn't write about this even on a slow news day.

In the west, stories of hell-raising celebrities are celebrated. They take pride in bad behavior; if you've never trashed a hotel room, you're not really a rock star. By contrast, Psy's supposedly rebellious antics are pretty tame. Example: he didn't study very hard, despite coming from a studious family. In Korea, this is newsworthy. An article from the October 10, 2012, online edition of *Munhwa Ilbo* ("Culture Daily") commented: "Psy had an Ugly Duckling kind of existence. He was the only member of his family who was a bad student. . . . His older sister never ranked lower than first in her class."

This reveals another cultural bias: in Korea, getting bad marks at school is tantamount to juvenile delinquency. It's also a direct act of disrespect toward one's parents, a core violation of Korean society's ethical system.

The article goes on to give equally unconvincing examples that Psy was a screw-up. You'll never guess what evil he was up to when he was seven years old: he stepped on the grass where there was a clear sign that said, "Don't step on the grass." According to the article, it was at this moment that Psy's mother decided, "I give up on my son."

Several Korean journalists and bloggers recounted the following anecdote, invariably expressing shock at Psy's horrible lack of filial piety: apparently, when Psy was still living at home, his father told him to quit smoking. Psy responded, "Why don't you quit first, Dad!"

Now, if this dialogue were taking place in an episode of the *Brady Bunch* or *Silver Spoons* or *Diff'rent Strokes* or some other moralistic, family-oriented American television sitcom, Psy's snappy remark would be followed by the father nodding and saying, "You know what? You're right. I should set a good example."

But in Korean society—back in the day, at least—a retort like Psy's could have resulted in the father telling the boy to stand on a chair, then whipping the kid's calves with his belt. That was a very common punishment among my classmates, usually reserved for very poor grades or very bad manners. Comparing welts the day after report cards were sent home was a popular recess pastime in my class. Sporadic stupidity, like a tasteless joke, was often met with a sharp flick on the kid's head by one of the parents, as though flicking off a tick. (The really serious punishments were usually meted out by the mother.)

In 2001, however, Psy's rebellion took a more serious turn when he was caught with marijuana. Psy's last words when he was being arrested for possession were, reportedly: "I guess I'll quit smoking now." Sources vary as to whether he was being serious or sarcastic. His father's reaction, however, was touching: "It looks like you're learning about the world now. I will believe in you even if you do something worse than this."

Two days after Psy's arrest, his beloved grandfather— who reportedly gave Psy his first taste of booze and his love of music—passed away. Psy, who missed the funeral because of his own incarceration, was inconsolable. "It was then that I became an adult," Psy told the Korean press.

You could say he made it up to his dad. Within less than two months of the "Gangnam Style" release, the stock value in his father's company doubled. It's hard to prove, but the surge is thought to be based on the investors' assumption that the father of such a successful son is probably running a successful business himself.

Most of Psy's songs are lighthearted, but there is one very serious one in his repertoire, called "Father." It's a heart-wrenching ode to his father, in which he sings that he's sorry he didn't understand that his dad was carrying the whole family on his shoulders.

No western pop icon would write a song about his or her parents, with the possible exception of Eminem's song "Cleanin' Out My Closet," which contains the line, "You selfish bitch, I hope you burn in hell for this shit."

Psy's career and his music are as good a symbol as any for old and new Korea—how the nation transformed in the space of a single generation, his and mine. So rapid was the transformation that a single person can be the entertainer who rules the Internet and yet have a touching song like "Father," expressing such self-flagellating, Confucian filial piety.

Psy will go down in history as the first real twenty-first-century entertainer: who else could combine Confucianism and farting?

# 3

# THE DYING ART OF SCHOOL THRASHINGS

. . . . . . . . . . . . . . . .

**QUESTION:** What's the connection between Starbucks and Confucianism?

**ANSWER:** There isn't any. That's the problem.

April 2013, Seoul. I am interviewing three government bureaucrats who represent the species I fear most in the world: Korean teachers.

Sitting on a stiff sofa in a somber room, I realize to my horror that all three of them are staring at my Starbucks cup. I start to panic.

I had fucked up.

I had totally forgotten that in Korea, food was to be eaten sitting and ideally indoors; you didn't walk around with an ice cream or a bottled water. And definitely not coffee. That would be like walking the streets with a pint of Guinness. The culture of carrying around a cup of coffee is very recent in Korea—a Starbucks invention. (I would say that's true for most of the world.) Who cares, you might well ask? Well, other than that it's considered slovenly to carry your drink around, I had also denied my hosts the chance to offer me a refreshment. I am appalled at myself. They do not know the protocol for what I have done. Neither do I. If they offer me coffee, I am obligated to say yes. If I refuse, they can't have any coffee either. That's the other Korean food etiquette hang-up: It's rude to eat in front of someone who is not eating.

Most people would have trouble understanding why I was being so neurotic about the passive-aggressive, silent Starbucks-staring contest going on between me and the education officials. I've made much worse gaffes, like the time I accidentally spilled hot soup on a Nobel laureate's lap and then set fire to his kitchen. But for me, the Starbucks faux pas reverberates because it represents irreconcilability between new and old Korea. The clash between convenience and good manners, for example. Overly roasted Seattle brew versus dishwater Nescafé. I had taken Korean modernization for granted: yes, change has been rapid, but this does not mean that everything modernized at the same rate.

Nowhere is this gap more apparent than in the Korean school system, which is why I was at the offices of the National Institute for International Education (NIIED), a governmental body affiliated with the ministry of education. I was expecting some kind of sleek glass pavilion, because I'd heard about all these exciting high-tech developments in the schools, such as the ministry's plan to replace all physical textbooks with e-readers by 2015.

So I was surprised to discover the building was in a sketchy part of town, and its dingy red exterior made it look like a Korean public bathhouse.

One of the first things my interviewees told me when I arrived was that they didn't want to answer my questions about the e-reader switchover. (I had submitted my interview questions in advance, per their request.) They didn't really give a reason except that they "couldn't give an objective opinion."

I would later discover that the e-reader program was a matter of controversy and that even within the government, some detractors were complaining that the switch was not worth the $2 billion price tag, and technology does not equal a good education.

Additionally, the officials I interviewed were crabby, imperious, and entitled (at several junctures they barked things like "stay focused on the topic" and "we don't have time for this question"), behavior that was consistent with what I had observed about my schoolteachers. I began to wonder whether these were bad signs—whether all the vaunted changes were overhyped. I had little faith in the Korean educational system's ability to evolve. In sixth grade, when I was studying a chapter in my Korean literature textbook about Marie Curie, my mother surprised me by quoting the first paragraph from memory. That story was in her sixth grade textbook, too.

Yet surely the system had to have been revamped; I could not imagine that the new Korea could get away with running its schools as it did when I was a student.

I'm of two minds about my Korean schooldays. On the one hand, the schools were Dickensian: marked by discipline, obedience, and relentless thrashings. I was so cowed by it that after three years, I transferred to an international school in Seoul, with my tail between my legs. On the other hand, this system is at the root of Korean success.

## THE SCIENCE AND ART OF THRASHING

The anchor of the Korean education system is the millennia-old Confucian belief that teachers are benevolent beings who guide you through your measly existence, and if you don't obey them, your life will be ruined. And this was no idle threat, given that your destiny was based on your performance on one exam—the university entrance exam.

There is no getting around it: my Korean teachers were the most arrogant, entitled people I've ever met in my life, and there's some pretty stiff competition out there. They were responsible for some pretty surreal childhood memories, including the multifarious, almost admirably creative thwacking. As a young student fresh from the United States, I wasn't prepared for how often this method would be meted out. We got hit for all kinds of reasons, crimes that have no name. Such as:

1. *Putting my hands in my pockets.* It was considered slovenly, or maybe the teachers suspected masturbation.
2. *Standing too casually during Monday morning assembly.* Ironically, this is known as the "at ease" military position.

3. *Wearing an unzipped jacket.* It had to be zipped all the way up or removed entirely. Unzipped outerwear was considered disheveled and redolent of corrupt influences like the Fonz from *Happy Days.*
4. *Having a U.S.-made pencil case.* Buying Korean-made goods was part of our duty in "helping Korea pay off its foreign debt"—that was the party line. The same line was used to explain why we weren't allowed to turn on the classroom lights: during daytime hours, we relied entirely on natural sunlight. The teachers never explained what this debt was all about, but we knew it was an embarrassment on the level of a national bedwetting.

The no-foreign-school-supplies rule was enforced by way of surprise inspections, heralded by the teacher suddenly yelling midlecture: "Everyone, put your hands on the top of your head!" This would send all the students into full-on freakout mode, trying in vain to hide their Japanese mechanical pencils in the gaps between the floorboards, like a drug dealer flushing his stash down the toilet.

In eighth grade, my teacher picked up a plastic Tupperware-type container from a student's bag, looked at the bottom, and shrieked, "Made in Thailand? Thailand?! If you're going to buy non-Korean goods, why would you pick a beggarly country like Thailand?" She then hit the offending student on the head with the contraband plastic container.

Even worse than getting hit was being responsible for someone else getting hit. On one occasion, I scored an 88 percent on a Chinese language exam—far exceeding any-one's expectations. Since I didn't speak Korean at the time and was regarded as the class idiot, the teacher announced, "Every student who scored lower than Hong Youn-kee [my Korean name] is going to get hit." I was not very popular after that.

Why so much brutality for such young children? For start-ers, Korean culture views childhood as an extremely high-stakes period. If you screw up your early years, you are finished, finished, finished. There's an old Korean saying that I heard often: "A habit begun at age three lasts until age eighty."

By the time you realize you might be in possession of bad habits, you are most likely past age three. Too late! You are already possibly doomed and have to work in constant emer-gency mode to outpace your demons. This early-instilled childhood panic was one reason why we were so obedient—and why it never really occurred to any of us to hit the teacher back.

People who have never experienced corporal punishment outside the home don't understand that it does not leave the same psychic scars as getting hit by your parents. Punishment from teachers was not personal, and if everyone is subjected to the same rules, you can tolerate quite a lot.

But some teachers were out of control. The most brutish teacher I ever had was my seventh-grade homeroom teacher, Mr. Chung—or Chung Sun-seng ("teacher"), to use the hon-orific. He was a very short, thin man of about thirty, with dark skin, poufy hair, eyes that darted quickly from side to side when he got angry, and a facial twitch. He had no neck and his trousers came up too high on his torso; these combined features made him look even smaller. Basically, he looked like a bad guy from a Roald Dahl children's book. And he should have been institutionalized.

At some point, a classmate's mother had called Chung Sun-seng to tell him to lay off a bit on the beatings where her own son was concerned. The next day, Chung Sun-seng called the boy and me to the hallway outside the classroom. The teacher boxed the boy's ears, saying, "Why'd you go crying 'Mommy, Mommy,' like a baby?" The boy fell to the ground; then the teacher kicked the boy repeatedly in the stomach and in the head until the boy bled from his mouth and lost a tooth.

Yes, I watched and did nothing. I don't remember what it was I was meant to have done, but I do remember that I was in trouble as well. All I could do was patiently wait my turn— but my turn never came. At the time, I thought it was because the teacher had run out of steam. Years later, I found out my mother had paid my teacher off, with an envelope full of cash, to leave me alone. I believe the teacher had called me out to witness this beating as a way of terrorizing me without physically harming me.

My mom is not a bribing sort of person, but paying off teachers was a normal practice. It still is. In the old days, a mother sliding an envelope to a teacher was a signal that she wouldn't mind terribly if the teacher were to do some creative grading on the next exam, maybe overlook a few wrong answers. The corruption was getting so out of hand that some schools, including mine, switched all the exams to multiple-choice bubble tests to be graded solely by computer.

Those tests were punitive. They weren't like the old SATs in the United States, where test takers had the unimaginable luxury of being able to use a number 2 pencil and—more crucially—an eraser to fix mistakes. We had to use a black felt-tip permanent marker. You couldn't change answers, and if you filled out the wrong bubbles for your student ID number or the subject test code, this would result in a grade of zero. The nicer teachers would sometimes issue you a new card, so long as you were willing to get hit for your mistake.

My eighth-grade homeroom teacher hit every single student in the class after exams. It wasn't because of overall poor performance. It was just something she always did. The number of times students got hit equaled the number of their class ranking in the exams: the top-scoring student got hit once; the second-ranking student got hit twice, and so on until the final student got hit sixty times. The teacher did it without an ounce of anger or vengeance. She said, "I'm being fair. Even the top student gets hit."

Corporal punishment in Korea has been phased out over the last decade, and it became officially illegal in 2011—but there are loopholes.[1] The laws only prohibit a teacher from striking a student directly, but it's technically still permissible for a teacher to ask students to punish themselves.

Yes, we would inflict pain on ourselves on command. If you've never seen this, and you happened to stroll by a classroom during one of these sessions, you probably would be puzzled by what you were looking at. You might wonder, "Why are sixty children holding their desks over their heads?"

My seventh-grade class had to do that for an hour or so because we lost the school choral contest. Sometimes we had to go outside to the gravel playground and do push-ups—not with our hands flat on the ground, but on our bare knuckles.

A popular punishment was *to ki dwim*, which means "rabbit run." To do the rabbit run, you crouch down into a low squatting position, grab onto your earlobes with your hands, and hop, hop, hop. Usually once or twice around the perimeter of the playground. It was amusing to watch if someone else was being punished but not if it was happening to you. And it's as good a piece of evidence as any that these teachers sometimes punished us for their own entertainment.

Corporal punishment has persisted in Korean schools for so long partly because the parents sanction it, and partly because the students think they deserve it.

Kim Young-sun, team director for the NIIED—and one of the bureaucrats whom I had embarrassed with the Starbucks cup—explained the parent-teacher complicity: "In the old days," she said, "the teacher was often much more educated than most of the parents. So the parents entrusted their children to the teachers. Some mothers would bring their own sticks to the teacher and say, 'Please use this to hit my child.'"

Apparently, such an instrument was called "the stick of love."

The weirdest instance I ever witnessed of a parent siding with a teacher over her own child was in seventh grade. During morning prep, my homeroom teacher, Chang Sun-seng—the tooth buster—called up a tall, thin girl to the front of the class. He said, "Your mother called me to tell me that she looked in one of your notebooks and found mean notes you had written about me." He smacked her across the face; the willowy girl lurched back from the blow.

Even the students supported the teachers' prerogative to hit them. In 2003—when corporal punishment was starting to disappear—a survey conducted by a Korean NGO representing teachers indicated that *fully 70 percent of Korean students said that corporal punishment was fair.*[2] The Korean newspaper *JoongAng Daily* reported at the time that students in the same survey said that the "honor" (I assume this means social status) of teachers had "eroded." But the real jaw dropper is that a third of the respondents "criticized themselves and their parents for not respecting teachers enough."

Students criticized themselves and their own parents, rather than the teacher? In other words, students felt that teachers could do no wrong.

This might sound like Stockholm syndrome, but it's much more complicated than that. The roots of teacher worship go back literally a thousand years.

## THE ARISTOCRACY EXAMS

Confucius, the Chinese sage who lived in the fourth century BC, was not just an author of fortune cookie quotes. His writings laid down a regimented system for making an orderly society out of chaos.

Confucianism didn't really get into full swing in Korea until its second wave—called neo-Confucianism—in the fourteenth century AD.

The rulers adopted neo-Confucianism partly as an excuse to overthrow the old aristocracy (with whom they were fed up). Under this new system, anyone could become an aristocrat. All they had to do was pass an excruciating civil service exam, called the *kwako*.[3]

In other words, the Korean political system was a meritocratic aristocracy—what an incredible oxymoron. A man from all but the very lowest classes had the right to sit for the *kwako* (originally instituted in the tenth century). Not only was it really hard, but it was also administered only once every three years. In a given exam year, only a hundred or so people would pass, out of thousands of applicants.

If you passed it, you were instantly given the title of *yangban*—you became an aristocrat. Not only that, but your whole family line was upgraded in the process. There's a catch, though. A big one. Your male heirs have to pass the *kwako* exam as well. If your descendants failed the exam three generations in a row, you and your family were stripped of the *yangban* title and went back to being nobodies. Does this not sound like something out of Grimms' fairy tales?

Ever since then, Korean students have been studying as if their lives, their family's lives, and the future lives of their entire bloodline depended on it. The *yangban* system technically disappeared at the end of the nineteenth century, but apparently, one hundred years is not long enough to shake off tradition. Confucianism in Korea is at the weakest point it's ever been, but it still has not completely released its hold on the education system.

How much has teacher worship changed in recent decades—between my school days and the present day? I can think of many examples of teachers abusing the power that society unquestioningly bestowed on them. But the government education officials I met seemed to think quite a lot had changed. They were proud of the abolition of corporal punishment, for example. And they said they had made significant strides in reducing the importance of rote memorization in favor of creativity.

They were obviously depressed, however, about the erosion of respect for teachers. Lee Dong-ho, the NIIED director, told me, "Compared to the past, students' parents are just as educated as the teacher, so there is a lot of friction between teachers and parents about the students."

The reason why Korean schoolteachers don't command as much respect as before is that for the last decade, Korean students have given their attention to private after-school learning centers, called *hakwons*. It's an open secret that students pay less attention to their public schoolteachers now because their *hakwon* studies have put them way, way ahead of the syllabus.

## PRIVATE TUTORING: THE KOREAN VICE

Private tutoring was illegal when I lived in Korea, punishable by fines for both the tutor and the family engaging them. Sometimes students would be caught because their fellow students ratted them out. When I was in the seventh grade, we had to fill out a questionnaire exposing our classmates. Questions included "Who is receiving private tutoring?" "Who is smoking?" and "Who is engaging in sexual intercourse?" My teacher told us we were obligated to write down names for every single question, whether we knew any guilty parties or not. If we left the questions blank, our own names would be inserted, he threatened.

The government viewed private lessons as a dangerous threat to the level playing field, as wealthy families would have a major advantage in getting their kids into top universities. The ban on private tutoring was officially lifted in the late 1990s, largely because it was impossible to enforce.

The legalization of private tutoring has proved a disaster. Korean parents throw money fanatically at *hakwons*. A family will typically pay anywhere from $1,000 to $4,000 per month per child for these extra after-school lessons. According to Kim Young-sun, 2.8 percent of the Korean GDP is spent on *hakwons*. To give a sense of how huge 2.8 percent is, that's over half of what Korea spends on its entire public K–12 education system.[4]

Some *hakwons* specialize in prepping students for the SAT exam required by U.S. universities. According to Sid Kim, who owns Wise Education, a respected and successful *hakwon*, some SAT summer prep courses offered by "ultra-elite" *hakwons* with "star teachers" charge $20,000. Just for the summer. Just for the SATs.

According a 2012 report on education issued by the Pearson publishing group, "The [Korean] government has become so worried about the extent of these studies that it has banned *hagwons* from being open after 10pm, but still needs to send out patrols to shut down those which mask illegal, after-hour teaching by posing as self-study libraries."[5]

In other words, there are study-easies. Like speakeasies, but for studyholics.

*Hakwons* disrupt one of the best aspects of Korean education: its meritocracy. "In Korea you can gain upward social mobility through public school education," Lee Dong-ho said. And this is why private tutoring really poses a problem: it favors families with money.

Another problem: there's something in the air at *hakwons* that gives rise to a surreal level of cheating and corruption. "In some ways, the shadiest business in Korea is the education business," says Sid Kim.

Case in point: In May 2013, the U.S. College Board canceled an SAT exam scheduled in Korea. It was the first time in the entire history of the College Board that it had canceled an exam for an entire country. The reason: mass cheating.

The cheating had occurred at over a dozen of Korea's *hakwons*. The *hakwon* teachers had illegally opened the tests the day before the exam and released the questions to the students.

According to Sid Kim, "The going rate for buying SAT answers is $10,000." To make the transaction look halfway legit, said Kim, the *hakwons* would claim they were offering "special private SAT sessions" for $1,000 an hour, for a minimum of ten hours. During these sessions the *hakwon* teacher would go over "sample" questions, which were in fact the actual questions for the real SAT exam.

Kim's *hakwon* was not implicated. In fact, he had already closed the SAT prep part of his business because he was being barraged by parents constantly and openly trying to bribe him for the SAT test answers. Kim, who has a PhD in education, has decided to close Wise Education for good, despite its profitability. "I'm leaving the business at the end of the year. Believe me, I love education, I've been doing it for eighteen years. I love working with kids. But I hate dealing with the Korean parents because they're shady."

Kim wasn't surprised by the SAT scandal at all. He said, "It's very simple economics. *Hakwons* make a ton of money [from selling answers], so ethics go by the wayside.

"I'd like to think I was one of the ones who tried to do it the right way," he added, "based on pedagogy and education, based on what's good for the student. I've pushed my way of doing things on the parents, but it's very difficult to convince them."

Kim believes the reason for Koreans' obsession with exam performance is based on Korea's ancient tradition of civil service exams. Today's Korean university exams have a much higher pass rate than the *kwako* exams of yore, but the stakes and stress level are still very high. Said Kim, "It's hard to change a mentality that has been going on for thousands of years."

University entrance anxiety is regarded as one of the

reasons that Korea has the highest suicide rate of any nation in the industrialized world. In fact, the most common cause of death for Koreans under the age of forty is suicide; for most other OECD nations, the leading cause is auto accidents or heart attack. Hanging is the most popular method, constituting 44.9 percent of all suicides; poison comes in at a close second.[6]

I would have guessed that jumping off buildings was the most popular method. At least, that's how we used to imagine our suicides when I was a student. We all thought about it. We all talked about it. One of my best childhood friends confessed to me, decades later, that she once stood atop her building and seriously contemplated jumping. Happily, she didn't go through with it.

When this suicide phenomenon comes up in conversation, people invariably ask me whether this is because suicide was considered a noble way of dealing with shame. No, it's not. You're thinking of medieval Japan.

Among the people I knew, academic pressure was the main reason for suicidal thoughts. When I was in school, the odds of university entrance were slim. In fact, you could only apply to one major university at a time, per year. If you failed the exam, you could take it the following year. But if you were a boy, you could only sit for the exam for up to three consecutive years before you had to enlist in the army. (If you were admitted to a university successfully, you could defer conscription until after you got your degree.)

By the time a man was done with his approximately two-year army stint, there was no way that he could have retained enough information ever to sit for the exam again. His life was finished.

According to Lee Dong-ho, as of 2008, Korea has been trying to implement a university admissions system "more similar to that of the United States, including volunteer work, hobbies, or activities in the application to show all their skills." But the plan has backfired: "This has the side effect of pressuring students to improve in [extracurriculars] in addition to test scores," says Kim Young-sun.

It's clearly not the teachers' or the government's fault. The students' and parents' obsession with competition borders on mental illness. In fact, according to the NIIED staff, the studying addiction has its own name in Korea: "study fever." Kim Young-sun sees this as a problem for Korea's future. "We have to keep up with the demands for creativity. When people are so focused on college, it's a loss of human resources. Korea loses its competitive advantage." I think it's very telling that even in the context of encouraging creativity, Kim still frames it in terms of Korea's national competitive edge.

Kim added that the ministry is also trying to de-emphasize rote memorization and the overly heavy importance placed on mathematics studies. While I would certainly not object to any education reforms that might lower the high Korean youth suicide rate, I think changes that threaten math and rote memorization are unfortunate. These are the aspects of my Korean education that I value most.

## SCARY MATH

South Korean students have almost invariably ranked number one in the world in terms of math aptitude, according to studies from multiple sources.[7] Imagine what it was like for me to enter this environment after being at a U.S. public school my whole life. In the Korean sixth grade, they were already studying advanced number theory. I was at a huge disadvantage: I was one of the few students in my class who couldn't add long columns of sums in their head.

I discovered this one day when my sixth-grade teacher, Hong *sun-seng* (no relation), suddenly started reading a series of numbers between two and four digits in length. I didn't know if he was reading phone numbers, or the Enigma code, or what. The students sat and listened intently until Hong *sun-seng* said, ". . . equals what?"

More than half the students answered with the correct sum of all those numbers. *They had done the sums in their heads.* No one had written anything down; he was calling out the numbers too quickly for that to have been feasible.

Was I watching a magic show?

As it turned out, the trendy after-school activity in those days was to go to a private learning academy for lessons in *amsan*—memory honing. This was one of the few types of *hakwon* that were legal in those days—because it taught content that was not directly related to any school subject.

The *amsan* academies are where students learned to do mental arithmetic. A small handful could do long columns of multiplication in their head as well. Apparently the trick (if you can call it that) is to first teach a student to be highly proficient in the use of the abacus. Then, whenever the instructor calls out numbers, you're supposed to envision the abacus beads flying around, and by seeing in your mind's eye the final position of the abacus beads, you are able to convert it to regular numbers, and you have your answer. Most complicated shortcut ever.

Private learning academies also pushed concentration exercises, with freaky consequences. A family friend had a daughter of about six, named Sujin. She had been attending a special "concentration academy." One night when our two families were dining at a Seoul restaurant, Sujin's parents asked her to do a demonstration: by focusing all her mental energy (or something), she was able to slice through a pair of wooden chopsticks with a business card. Without denting the card. My sisters and I could not believe our eyes, so Sujin did it again and again.

One aspect of Korean school I did appreciate is that girls studied as much as boys. They didn't have this hang-up that American girls have that boys won't like them if they show talent in math and science. Korean guys are not especially attracted to girls who are bad at math and science.

## THE ASH EATERS

My parents knew students when they were in school who learned English by memorizing one page of a dictionary each day. After they'd fully committed it to memory, they'd burn it and eat the ashes. This wasn't because they really thought the words would stay in their body if they ate the pages. Burning a page is a ritual sacrifice symbolizing what you have to forego—time, your short-term happiness—in order to achieve something more important. Such practices are very infrequent and largely anecdotal—everyone knows someone who knows someone who has done it. But the legend has staying power because it symbolizes the real suffering and masochism involved in assimilating huge amounts of information.

My favorite anonymous Korean American author of the blog "Ask a Korean" puts it best: "The Korean [he refers to himself thusly, in the third person] cannot see why 'rote memorization' became a dirty word in education somehow. . . . There are certain things about contemporary America that drive The Korean crazy, and this is one of them: The idea that the process of learning is somehow supposed to be fun. Just drop it. Forget it. What is fun is the result of learning— the infinite amount of fun when you finally put the finished product to use."

That said, I disagreed with my Korean teachers as to what kinds of information need to be committed to memory. For example, I don't think it was really necessary to make us memorize the Beaufort wind scale, which is a nineteenth-century method of measuring wind speed, on a seventeen-point scale, by how choppy the water is. That was in seventh or eighth grade. Unless you are a sailor with not even the most basic technology for measuring wind speed, you will never, ever need to use this. And if you do need to use it, you can probably look it up. Like, in a book or on a computer.

We also had to learn a rock density scale by heart. For example, limestone's density ranges from 1.93 to $2.90 \, \mathrm{g/cm^3}$; the exam tested our knowledge on such data for a dozen or so other rock types. I'm sure this information will come in handy the next time I find myself trapped in a limestone quarry.

My memorization skills were so well honed at Korean school that it's now become an involuntary and automatic reflex. I have almost perfect recall of conversations I've had going back about twenty years or so. If required, I can recite an entire thirty-minute exchange verbatim. Sometimes this is useful, as when I'm arguing with a male companion about whether one of us did or did not break some previously made promise. However, my gift of recall is very annoying to other people. They forgot to tell us at Korean school that memory does not lead to a happy life.

Annoying or not, being trained in rote memorization, along with discipline, obedience, worship of authority, and good old-fashioned terror of failing is one of the cornerstones of Korea's accelerated success.

Cosmetically, a lot has changed in Korean schools. Class sizes are a great deal smaller—around thirty-two students; in my day, it was sixty. Corporal punishment is gone. Schoolrooms actually turn on their electric lighting. Most schools reintroduced uniforms, ending the open-attire policy of my day, which was really fortunate, since the latter was a charade. All students, regardless of gender, take both home economics and technology. Korea was the first nation in the world to install Internet access in 100 percent of all primary, middle, and high schools.[8] The surprise inspections for foreign school supplies have been rendered unnecessary by Korea's wealth, plus the fact that Korean-made school products are now quite excellent.

# 4

# CHARACTER IS DESTINY: THE WRATH OF HAN

· · · · · · · · · · · · · · · ·

"[KOREANS] ARE THE CRUELEST, MOST RUTHLESS people in the world," wrote Ian Fleming in *Goldfinger*, adding that Koreans have no respect for human life. In this scene, the supervillain of the title is explaining to James Bond why he picked only Koreans as bodyguards, among whom is the stocky, grunting, subhuman karate expert Oddjob, who decapitates people by hurling his razor-sharp black bowler hat at them.

Fleming's description of Koreans is regarded as widely racist, but my desire to be offended is contradicted by a sheepish "How did he know?" sort of feeling.

In order to understand the Korean drive that propelled the country to wealth, you have to know that Korea has been the whipping boy of fate for five thousand years. The peninsula has been invaded four hundred times in its history, and it has never once invaded any other nation, unless you count its participation in the Vietnam War.[1]

The result of all this abuse is a culturally specific, ultra-distilled form of rage, which Koreans call *han*. I usually find it pretentious when someone says that a particular word is untranslatable, but *han* really is untranslatable.

By definition, only Koreans have *han*, which arises from the fact that the universe can never pay off this debt to them, not ever. (Koreans are not known for being forgiving.)

*Han* is never-ending. It is not ordinary vengeance. As Korean film director Park Chan-wook (*Oldboy, Stoker*) told me, "*Han* only occurs when you cannot achieve proper vengeance, when your vengeance is not successful." (It is worth mentioning, however, that Park emphatically denies that his movies are about *han*.)

My mom describes *han* this way: "When sad things happen not by your own design but by fate, and over a long period of time." I asked her to give me examples of *han*. They were grim: "If a baby is abandoned by his parents and suffers throughout his childhood because there is no one to take care of him, then he feels *han* toward his parents. If a woman gets married young and her husband abandons her for another woman and leaves the wife no money, and the wife has to live a life of strife, then she builds up *han* toward her husband and herself. And finally, Koreans have *han* toward the Japanese."

But Koreans do not consider *han* to be a drawback. It's not on the list of traits they want to change about themselves.

The word *han* came up several times during the course of my interviews for this book. When I asked the co-creator of the popular Korean soap opera *Winter Sonata*, Kim Eun-hye, why Korean dramas contained so much human misery, she said, "Well, you know, Koreans have a lot of *han*." When I asked a top music executive why old Korean songs were so sad, he said, "Koreans have a lot of *han*."

It's the opposite of karma. Karma can be worked off from life to life. With *han*, the suffering never lessens; rather, it accumulates and gets passed on. Imagine the story of Job, except when God gives him a new family and new riches, he has to relive his suffering over and over again.

One enduring example of the persistence of *han* is Korea's emblematic song—not the national anthem, but the song that represents Korea more than any other: a folk song called "Arirang." It's so old that no one really knows how old it is. It's so universally Korean, in fact, that even North Koreans play it on their news broadcasts and consider it a symbol of their nation, too. The gigantic mass spectacle North Korea hosts every year is called the Arirang Games.

What is this song about? In verse one, a spurned lover says, "Ye who hast tossed me aside and left me, I hope you get a foot disease before you have traveled ten li." (The subsequent stanzas are more conventional love declarations.)

That first stanza is spiteful and vengeful. And it speaks volumes that Koreans have used "Arirang" as their international ambassadorial song, without any discussion about changing the lyrics. They don't question whether it's okay to air this kind of hostility in public.

*Han* reminds me of Carl Jung's concept of racial memory—the idea that the collective experiences of a race are hereditary. Thus, the memories of our ancestors are encoded in our DNA, or at least in our unconscious. The neuroses the current generation endures is because of the suffering of their ancestors.

*Han* doesn't just mean that you hate people who have wronged you for generations. It also means that random people in your life can spark the flame of *han*. Someone who cuts you off in traffic or disappoints you with his or her friendship can unleash the anger of generations. I have never seen so many roadside fistfights, or so many people permanently shunning their friends, as in Korea.

Some claim that one can die from *han*. The disease caused by *han* is called *hwa-byong* in Korean, which literally means "anger illness." *Hwa-byong* is an actual, medically recognized condition. It is listed as a "culturally specific disease" in Appendix 1 of the *Diagnostic and Statistical Manual of Mental Disorders*, fourth edition (DSM-IV).

What I found astonishing in the course of researching this book is that many Koreans ascribe Korean success to *han*. It makes sense, in a way. A race that has been under constant threat knows it can survive anything.

The degree to which the Japanese and Koreans hate each other is dumbfounding. The animosity is at least six hundred years old.

Korea's more recent grievances against Japan stem from the fact that Japan invaded Korea and colonized it from 1910 to 1945. During this time, Japan famously forced Koreans into involuntary manual labor; thousands of Korean women were forced to become "comfort women"—sex slaves of Japanese military officers. (The Japanese government officially apologized in 1993, but in December 2012, Prime Minister Shinzo Abe threatened to retract the apology.)

It was illegal for Korean schools to use the Korean language in the classroom. Koreans had to take on Japanese names —my surname would have been Tokuyama if the Axis nations had won World War II. Until 1992, Korean nationals living in Japan had to report to the immigration authorities and get fingerprinted every six months—even though one's fingerprints don't change every six months.

In fact, hating the Japanese might be the only thing that North and South Koreans have in common.

Against all odds, North and South Korea have started unofficially cooperating to get Japan to stop claiming sovereignty over the Liancourt Rocks, a tiny pair of islands between Korea and Japan, in the Sea of Japan.

As the name suggests, the Liancourt Rocks are literally two large volcanic rocks and a few dozen smaller rocks that are barely big enough for a seagull to land on. The total surface area is 46 acres (0.19 square kilometers). They are known as Takeshima in Japan, and as Dokdo in Korea. Obviously, I'm going to refer to them hereafter as Dokdo.

How small is Dokdo? Well, the very biggest of the islands, the West Islet, is so small (21.9 acres: 0.09 square kilometers) that if the terrain were completely flat, you could walk from one end of the island to the other in five minutes. Except that it's not flat; it's basically all cliff, and it's very windy.

How habitable are these rocks? Consider: in the year 2 BC, the Roman emperor, Augustus, was so horrified by his daughter Julia's disgraceful and public adultery that he gave her the worst punishment he could think of, barring execution. He banished her to the island of Trimerius. Which is three times bigger than the Dokdo West Islet.

Which is to say that Dokdo is theoretically too hostile even to be a Roman penal colony. And yet a few Koreans live there voluntarily. Their *han* keeps them alive.

Dokdo had no official permanent residents until 1981, when a Korean octopus fisherman living in nearby Ulleung Island was so incensed by Japan's continuing claims on Dokdo that *he made his permanent home there.*

A handful of Koreans choose to live there—no more than four in total at any given time—purely as a patriotic gesture. Furthermore, over six hundred Koreans have registered their official address in Dokdo, though they do not physically inhabit the island. This practice arose from the National Dokdo Permanent Address Registration Movement.[2] The island is also patrolled at all times by a fleet of about thirty-seven Korean police.

Meanwhile, Japanese residents started registering there in 2005. But not a single one of them actually set up home on the island. That's the difference between Korea and Japan in terms of their respective determination to claim the islands as their own.

Dokdo is to Japan and Korea what Alsace-Lorraine was to France and Germany—if Alsace-Lorraine were a tiny burp of skipping stones surrounded by a sea, hit with year-round gusts, and basically uninhabitable. Japan and Korea have been fighting over Dokdo since the fifteenth

century, despite the fact that apparently the rocks are erod-
ing. What's at stake? Well, natural gas deposits, fishing rights—
and pride.

Korea claims that Japan lost Dokdo to Korea as part of
its surrender agreement to the Allies at the end of World
War II. Japan claims that the Treaty of Peace with Japan—
signed in 1951—did not mention Dokdo as part of the colonized territories that Japan was expected to relinquish.
Wisely, other countries don't really want to get involved in this
turf war.

At my elementary school in Korea, I learned a children's
song called "Dokdo Is Our Land." It's catchy. The first verse
goes, "There is a lonely island 200 li southeast of Ulleung
Island that birds call their home. No matter how much
someone claims this is their land, Dokdo is our land." All five
verses to the song end with "Dokdo is our land." I think there's
a subtle message in there somewhere.

In 2008, new editions of Japanese textbooks declared
Takeshima to be a Japanese territory. For Koreans everywhere, this was the last straw (or the first of many last straws,
as it would turn out).

And it was this tiny pile of pebbles that led to a miracle of
miracles: on November 13 of that same year, twenty-odd
North and South Korean representatives convened at a hotel
in Pyongyang to hold the Inter-Korean Forum to Oppose
Japan's Distorted History and Japan's Maneuver to Rob
Dokdo.

As Reuters aptly wrote at the time, "It took six decades
for the divided Koreas to meet to talk about Japan's colonial

past, but it took them just two hours to agree they had common grievances with their Asian neighbor."[3]

As someone told me, "Is it really a coincidence that every time North Korea tests missiles, it always happens to be over Japan?"

On December 4, 2012, North Korea's official news agency, KCNA, published a blistering editorial against Japan's claim to Dokdo, saying, "In view of Japan's sovereignty claim over Dokdo, we would like to say that we are taking explicit steps." Then, on December 12, North Korea launched a three-stage rocket, the Unha-3 (which it called a "satellite"). It conveniently crossed over Japan's Okinawa prefecture before landing in the sea near the Philippines.

Hilariously, South Korea and Japan always jointly condemn North Korea's missile tests. I feel there have to be at least a few South Koreans who are crossing their fingers behind their backs when making these kinds of statements.

In 2008, one prominent Korean intellectual wrote a controversial op-ed saying that South Korea should allow North Korea to build a missile base on Dokdo, and that South Korea should help subsidize it.[4]

Dokdo is just one example of Japanese-Korean animosity. More massive bickering between the two nations occurred in 1996, when FIFA—the international soccer regulatory body—made the unprecedented move of granting the two nations cohosting rights for the 2002 World Cup.

Clearly, FIFA officials had no idea about Japanese-Korean relations; otherwise they would never have agreed to this.

Once the two nations won their bid, it was just about the last decision they were able to agree on. The first nightmare was what the cup would be called. Japan and Korea fought over whether it would be called the Japan-Korea World Cup or the Korea-Japan World Cup. In theory, it should have been Japan-Korea because, alphabetically, Japan comes before Korea. But Korea won that argument. According to rumor, this was part of a compromise between the two countries: Korea's name would appear first and Japan would get to host the crucial final match.

To drive the point home, some Korean World Cup paraphernalia spelled Korea with a *C*: Corea. (I have a red World Cup souvenir towel to prove it.) "Corea" is not the word for Korea in either English or French. It's Spanish, which is not an official FIFA language.

In fact, I've even heard Koreans make the claim, which I find highly dubious, that Korea really is supposed to be spelled with a *C*, and that Japan forcibly changed the first letter to a *K* so that Japan would always come first alphabetically.

During the tournament, some matches were held in Japan; some in Korea. The players had to fly back and forth between the countries. It was deeply annoying for everyone. FIFA realized its initial error of judgment, and in 2004 made it illegal for multiple countries to cohost the World Cup.

When I first moved to Korea, the country had been independent of Japan for forty years. But the bile was still there.

I also soon discovered that some of the Korean vocabulary I knew was not actually Korean; it was Japanese. Not only that, I was not allowed to use these words. One of the first phrases my parents taught my sisters and me when we started school in Korea was, "I have to go to the *byonso*." *Byonso*, meaning "toilet," was a Japanese word, a leftover from the colonial area. One of my sisters said this to the teacher on the first day of school, and the teacher corrected her, saying pointedly, "You mean, you have to go to the *hwajangshil*"—the latter being the Korean and politically correct term.

Many Korean kids I grew up with, myself included, had an inferiority complex when it came to Japan. I mean, any kid could plainly see that Japanese mechanical pencils were much better than Korean ones, which broke all the time. The Japanese lunchboxes were compact and retained heat; the Korean ones were bulky and your lunch was always cold by midday.

My favorite rock bands always toured Japan; however, these bands never performed in Seoul (with the exception of Duran Duran).

What does this have to do with the Korean Wave, you ask? Though many Koreans would not like to admit it, a lot of their drive and motivation arose from a desire to beat Japan at something, anything. In the 1980s, all of Asia had benchmarked Japan as the nation to aspire to economically. Currently, only Korea is succeeding. And *han* has a lot to do with it. In the late 1990s, Samsung had set its sights on the Japanese electronics giant Sony as the company to beat. Not IBM, not Microsoft, not Apple, but Sony.

## BODY AND SOIL ARE NOT TWO

Like many Koreans, my parents are guilty of what I would call "nature fetishism." They're not the only ones; Rousseau had an idealized notion of the "noble savage," for example, and Thoreau wanked on about Walden Pond while having his mom do his laundry.

I can't begin to count how many times I was on some kind of trip with my parents and they woke me up at dawn because it was mandatory that I watch the fucking sunrise.

This gets at the heart of two least-favorite pastimes: waking up early and nature fetishism. The two are intertwined.

In Korea, I genuinely got the feeling that sleeping late was kind of a sin. It was considered slovenly. I wasn't even allowed to sleep in on nonschool days. Koreans are very into the idea that the body cycles should be in harmony with the natural environment. Thus, it was against nature not to wake with the sun.

According to an ancient Korean proverb, *Shin to bul ee*: "Body and soil are one."[5] In other words, humans are basically an agricultural product, literally coming from the earth. Though this saying has no connection with Judeo-Christianity, it has some parallels with the biblical notion of God making Adam from the earth. It's a concept that predates Confucianism or any official organized belief, which is why this idea seems incongruous with what Seoul looks like today— jam-packed skyscrapers with very little open space. The westerner in me finds this hard to stomach. I'm in agreement with something Woody Allen once said: "Nature and I are two."

In a way, "body and soil are one" is a powerful anti-intellectual sentiment. It implies that the body has supremacy over the mind. It's exactly the opposite of Descartes's famous dictim: "I think, therefore, I am"—which is the very foundation of modern western culture.

Much of this body-and-soil philosophy has its roots in shamanism. Like many modern, westernized Koreans, I had always thought shamanism was some embarrassing part of Korea's primitive past, practiced only by the illiterate.

Up to 80 percent of modern-day Icelanders "cannot completely rule out the possibility that elves exist"—according to various polls. When I first heard that, about five years ago, I laughed incredulously and thought there must be something really wrong with Iceland.

So imagine my shock when Lee Charm, head of the Korean Tourism Organization, told me that the same proportion of Koreans—up to 80 percent—adhere to the ancient beliefs of shamanism in some form. He added that there are now fifty-five thousand practicing shamans in Korea—"more than the clergy of all the other religions put together."

Shamanism is linked to animism, the belief that everything has a spirit, rather than the idea of transcendent gods, and it is the most primitive form of religion in the world. Druids, for example, had similar beliefs.

In premodern Korea, before the tenth century, shamanism was the closest Korea had to a religion—but basically it was mostly a loose agglomeration of female witches and soothsayers who communicated with spirits and demons in order to cast spells for good luck. People paid them loads of money to chant for hours or even days, to bring everything from good crops to conceiving a baby.

Not shockingly, shamans—called *mudang* in Korean—are often viewed as mentally ill women. They sometimes channel spirits in their rituals. I've heard from semireliable sources that some shamans claimed to have channeled General Douglas MacArthur, who is considered a hero by many Koreans because he led the UN forces in a triumphant attack that saved Seoul from being captured by the North Koreans. This does not, however, explain why old shaman women would up the ante on their hustle by donning MacArthur's trademark sunglasses and corncob pipe.

I think it's fair to say that a lot of Koreans don't really want shamanism to be part of modern Korea. In fact, shamanism was made illegal in Korea in the fourteenth century, and did not start to become legal again until the late twentieth century—and even then, only in certain regions.

I had a hard time finding anyone in Korea who was willing to discuss shamanism on the record until I came across an American, David A. Mason, who is a professor of Korean cultural tourism at Gyeongju University and a longtime expat in Korea. A self-professed atheist, he's been making an academic and personal study of shamanism in Korea for decades.

When Mason told me more about shaman rituals I couldn't see how anyone could help but find it embarrassing and stupid. According to Mason, the basic shamanistic belief is the *sanshin*—the mountain spirit. "In my home town there are shaman shrines where the woman advertises she got her powers from a certain holy mountain man that she can call upon. It's a big sales point."

In essence, shamanism is the belief that all happiness stems from harmony with nature. Says Mason, "If we have bad health or bad luck, it means there's some mistake in our relationships, either to nature, to other people, ancestors, or the spirits." Traditionally, a shaman ceremony could last up to seventy-two hours. Shamans would offer concrete advice, such as "Move the tomb of your ancestor."

There are no clear figures on how many shamans continue to operate or how much they charge, because it's still largely illegal and unregulated. Most areas that have lifted restrictions on shamans are remote. "They can run you through the ringer if you're the client," says Mason. "Surely, [rates go] from hundreds of dollars up to thousands quite easily, and we hear rumors that for a rich person, the really great shamans do it night and day, and get a million dollars for this."

As for what a shaman ritual looks like, that runs the gamut as well. "For some short sessions," Mason said, "you just sit with the shaman in front of a big boulder or in front of a pine tree." Mason confirmed that some modern business owners, when opening a new store or location, occasionally hire shamans to hold a traditional good-luck ceremony to anoint the new space. "They don't want the public hearing a rumor that their business is going to have bad fortune, so instead they want to spread the rumor that a shaman has been there." These business-site rituals are sometimes conducted with a dead pig or a pig's head on a stake.

Mason pointed out that as much as Koreans want to bury their shaman roots, the influence of this faith is still very apparent today.

In recent decades, the biggest enemies of shamanism have been Korea's many fervent Christians. Which, said Mason, is highly ironic, since Korean Christianity is rather shamanistic.

If you've ever been to some of these churches in Korea, you know exactly what he's talking about. Even at some churches of "mainstream" denominations, like Presbyterianism, people can be seen going into a trance and speaking in tongues.

An important aspect of Korean Christianity that has its roots in shamanism, said Mason, is that Korean Christians pray for real-world benefits in a way that far exceeds their western counterparts. "The major religions—Christianity, Judaism, Islam—are supposed to make you a better person"— not a wealthier person.

Another huge irony is that shamanistic rites crept into Confucian practices, even though it was the Confucian rulers who stamped out shamanism in the first place. Most notably, the rituals associated with ancestor worship—*jae sa*. Or as I like to call it, picnicking with the dead. At least twice a year, my family would take a long drive to the family gravesite, and we'd conduct these rituals I didn't understand. We would burn incense in an urn in front of the graves, then pour alcohol into a separate urn—sometimes rice wine, sometimes red wine. Then one by one, we'd bow to the dead. Then we would lay out food and have a picnic right by the tombs, which I found morbid and kind of inappropriate. Only when I was much older was I told that we were literally supposed to be acting as if the dead were eating with us.

Shamanism doesn't fit in very smoothly with Korea's modern ambitions. Neither does the whole "body and soil are one" nature fetishism. First of all, Seoul has very little in the way of green space, despite impressive recent improvements. The air is polluted. And as for the belief that harmony with nature leads to happiness, how do you explain the fact that, as mentioned in the previous chapter, South Korea has the highest suicide rate of any country in the industrialized world?

One reason may be that Korean culture is very skeptical about mental illness. Aside from traditional fear that insanity is a type of demon possession, which is a universal concept, Koreans also believe that depression and schizophrenia come from being misaligned with nature—an ancient, animistic holdover—which is another way of saying that it's the victim's fault.

What it comes down to is this: Racial depression is okay. Individual depression is not okay.

Another reason for the high suicide rate is that Koreans are unforgiving of failure, an attitude that has contributed both to success and misery. As much as Koreans love their rural nostalgia, they are no match for a thousand years of Confucianism in Korea.

## CONFUCIANISM, THE MOST STRESSFUL BELIEF SYSTEM ON EARTH

Let me give you an example of why I always had such a hard time passing for a real Korean. One central tenet of etiquette in Korea is that you have to pay attention to who you are in relation to those around you: Man or woman? Older or younger? Professional rank? Etc., etc. You base all of your actions on hierarchy. In fact, this is the reason why it is never considered rude to ask someone's age—technically, you ask when they were born. Without knowing which party is older, no one knows how to act or speak.

If someone new enters the room, you have to recalibrate your behavior. It's part of being Korean. But for me, it never came naturally. I was twelve when we moved to Korea; that is way too old to learn.

I always felt that interacting with people in Korea is like being in one of those Hollywood movies in which FBI agents or spies have to raid a house to arrest a gang of criminals. The agents might enter the front door with the best attack plan in the world, but every time they enter a new room, there's a brand-new set of data they have to take in, on the basis of which they have to make split-second decisions: Is there anyone else in the room? Armed or unarmed? Where are they in the room? Do you need your night vision goggles? Are the members of your team situated such that no one's back is exposed?

Stressful, huh? Welcome to the daily heart attack that I experience every time I visit Korea.

The reason you have to go through this whole rigmarole is based on the Confucian concepts of keeping order by everyone knowing their place in the social hierarchy, being respectful of those superior to them, and not rocking the boat.

The Chosun Dynasty adopted Confucianism in all walks of civil and personal life at the beginning of the fifteenth century. The nation's kings were worried about losing power and sought a drastic solution to obliterate the two biggest threats: chaotic class warfare and the increasingly influential Buddhist clerics. Since the system favored those already in power, it was a no-lose proposition for the monarchs.

Several business books have speculated that the modern-day Korean economic miracle has Confucianism to thank. This is certainly possible, since unquestioning obedience certainly can be a huge time-saver when you're trying to build an economic empire.

Lee Charm, head of the Korean Tourism Organization, gave an excellent definition of Confucianism. "It goes back to the relationship between heaven and earth, spiritual and physical. It's a set of behavioral rules based on an observation of nature, an observation of the relationship between plants, animals, and the cosmos."

Lee was born Bernhard Quandt in the western German city of Bad Kreuznach, and he visited Korea for the first time in 1978, when he was in his midtwenties. He was supposed to stay only six months; instead, he went completely native.

Lee learned flawless Korean, married a Korean woman, and in 1986 became a Korean national. He gave himself a Korean name. For his surname, he adopted Lee, his wife's family name. His first name, Charm (the r is silent), is the Korean word for "cooperate" or "participate"—a badge of pride for his role in Korean society. He is a businessman and local celebrity. He acts in the occasional Korean television drama, and by happy coincidence, he once portrayed a real-life historical figure whose life closely paralleled his own: the Prussian aristocrat Paul Georg von Möllendorf, who in the late nineteenth century settled in Korea and became a special adviser to Korea's King Gojong. Möllendorf adopted traditional Korean court dress and chose a Korean name, Mok In-dok, and was instrumental in helping form Korean foreign policy.

This storyline mirrors what Lee is doing now. In 2009, then-president Lee Myung-bak appointed Lee Charm as the country's first non-Korean-born head of the national tourism board. It's a highly important post in Korea, a central part of the overall Korean brand management. It's shocking that an extremely tall, white German guy with very Teutonic features would be appointed to lead it, considering that Korea, the so-called Hermit Kingdom, was once so afraid of westerners.

Charm's assimilation into Korean society at the height of its cold war xenophobia in the 1970s and 1980s makes him, from my point of view, a very reliable expert on the idea of what it means to be Korean.

Lee believes that Confucianism took a wrong turn somewhere on the journey from theory to practice: Korea's ancient rulers corrupted Confucianism and turned it into a political tool. "Confucianism in Korea became very pharisaical. The original idea was very good. The husband has a certain role;

the wife has a certain role. But their relationship is not [supposed to be] top down; originally, they're on equal footing."

As mentioned, women in modern Korea were not allowed to be the legal head of the household until 1990. So I was surprised to learn that until the fifteenth century, women had equal rights. "They could be head of the household, and they could be the master of the ancestral ceremonies," said Lee. In other words, there was really no reason why the women in my family had to bow before the graves twice as many times as the men.

"[The current practice that] the parents decide everything or the husband decides everything is a misinterpretation of the Confucian concept," Lee explained. He has very good reasons for his surprisingly frank views on the matter. He suffered the raw end of the system when he started dating the Korean woman who became his wife. When he first came to Korea in 1978, it was unthinkable for a Korean to marry a foreigner. It's more acceptable now but still frowned upon.

In Confucianism as practiced in Korea, a person's identity is determined by the male side of the family. Your ancestry is recorded in a *hojok*, a record of lineage. Traditionally, a non-Korean male could not be in the *hojok*, nor could any of his descendants. Using the same logic, illegitimate children could not be in the *hojok* unless the father declared his paternity. These *hojok* restrictions were not completely eliminated until 2005; it took three more years to officially implement the change.[6] So what, you ask? Why did your name have to be written in some silly book?

The *hojok* was not merely ceremonial; it wasn't like *De-*

*brett's Peerage* in the UK or a social register that tracks descendants of the *Mayflower* in the United States. In Korea, if you were not in the *hojok*, you did not exist as a Korean citizen. You had about as much status as an illegal immigrant. You could not inherit your parents' assets after their death. It would be difficult to find a job.

One Korean American adoptee who suffered the cruelty of the old *hojok* system is Daniel Gray. The story of his life illustrates how much Korea has and has not changed.

Today, Gray is director of marketing and tours at O'ngo Food Communications in Seoul, a company that offers food tours and Korean cooking classes to international chefs. Though he seems perfectly natural in his current milieu, he has actually only been living in Korea as an adult for the past seven years.

He was born in Korea, out of wedlock: "My mother and father were in love," he said, but his father was already married with three kids—a serious problem for their son. This was the mid-1980s, when illegitimate children had no legal status. "My mother would not have been able to register me as a person, not even under her own family line, because she was not a man. There was a lot of social stigma against [illegitimate children]. All the schools would have known I didn't have a father. It would be hard to get into university.

"My mother begged my father to take me in, because of the *hojok*," he said. His father did take him in for a while, but "my stepmother didn't care for me much at all," Daniel recalls.

One day, Daniel was told that his mother was coming to pick him up. But the woman who showed up at his father's home was not his mother. She was a representative from the Holt orphanage—Korea's most established orphanage and adoption agency, founded in 1955 by American Christian missionaries. "She took me to a noodle restaurant and a toy store and brought me a change of clothes. I was upset, I didn't exactly know what was happening."

What had happened was that Daniel's father and stepmother declared that they were not going to take care of Daniel anymore, so his mother put him up for adoption. Daniel was six years old at the time.

Daniel was only at the orphanage for three months. "I was very lucky," he said, recalling that any day a kid at the orphanage got adopted was an exciting one. The adoptee "would get a gift box from their [new] parents. It would always have a picture book and chocolate, so all the kids would look forward to that. There would be a big party, and everyone would get snacks and candy."

Daniel's gift box included photos of his new family and home. "All the pictures were very foreign," he said. "I saw pictures of my parents' house, a two-story house with a big front yard. And my father had an orange Ford truck up front." There were also photos of his adoptive parents, Linda and Larry Gray, as well as his new little sister, another Korean orphan who had previously been adopted by the family.

It took a long time before Daniel thought of the Grays as his parents. "I didn't speak for a long time," he said. "I had a lot of major health problems and needed a lot of dental work." The adjustment was rocky. "I was very distant, very scared." He was also mistrustful. The Grays tried to introduce Daniel to Korean American friends as well as to a Korean minister, but "When I first got to America I was really scared they were going to send me back, so I disassociated as much as possible." This included forgetting all his Korean.

Despite a rebellious childhood and adolescence, Daniel excelled at school, at art, and at the guitar. He became a writing teacher and a volunteer at inner-city schools in Wilmington. But he felt restless. At age twenty-six, he went to Korea to take a job teaching English at a small school in the southern city of Gyeongju.

After two years, he gathered the courage to go to Seoul and try to find his birth mother. It was a logistical nightmare. "The process of finding your parents is not very well detailed," he recalled. "There is a lot of misinformation." It's a good thing he didn't wait too long to embark on his search: "The agencies that helped me five years ago no longer exist." Not only that, his original orphanage, the missionary-run Holt group, no longer helps orphans locate their birth parents. Nowadays orphans have to go through a third party to locate their adoption records.

The reason for this red tape is horrifying: "There are a lot of anti-adoption groups," he said, "groups that feel that the orphans should not have been put up for adoption in the first place. They say, the parents weren't properly vetted." So institutions make it difficult for children to find their birth parents, a situation that only serves to punish the innocent.

Finally, Daniel went through Holt. "They opened up my file. They sent a letter to my mother." Two weeks later, she replied that she wanted to meet her son. In fact, that was why she made sure she left her address with Holt from the beginning: "She was waiting for me," Gray recalls.

The long-awaited reunion happened at the Hapjeong train station in Seoul; Daniel's biological mother had come in from her hometown.

"She gave me a big hug and said, *'Oreh gan man i eh yo.'*" Which means, "It's been a long time."

"She asked me how I was, if I was healthy. She asked what I was doing." She also told him his real age: he was one year older than he was led to believe. When his birth mother put Daniel up for adoption, she knocked a year off his age, thinking that a younger child might stand a better chance of getting adopted.

Daniel chose to stay in Korea, which is a very brave thing to do, given the country's hostile climate toward Korean adoptees. Illegitimate children now have legal status without the declaration of paternity, but a lot of Koreans are uncomfortable with his western last name. "There are still repercussions," he said. "Some Koreans still see it as a negative. Some of the parents of girls I dated in the past thought I wasn't a whole person," he said.

Yet even with all those impediments, Gray says he feels Korean. "I feel more comfortable here," he said. Now he is a successful businessman in Seoul, has relearned Korean, and is about to marry a Korean woman. He plans to take his birth mother to Delaware to meet his adoptive parents. "She said it was a dream of hers, to thank them."

Daniel's story makes it obvious how fortunate it is that some aspects of Confucianism have disappeared. Other aspects have eroded more subtly: I've noticed that young people no longer have the universal, automatic reflex of offering their seat to an elderly person. In my day (yes, I know how crotchety that sounds), kids would literally grab the hand of an old person, even a total stranger, and escort them to the seat they were yielding.

I've also begun to see young people yell at older people, including a strange thirty-something woman in the Seoul subway who was wearing a green cellophane sun visor and a lot of makeup. She was screaming shrilly that my parents were monopolizing the station manager with a question. I can say with complete confidence that I never witnessed any such incident when I was growing up in Seoul.

These might seem like harsh descriptions of the Korean character. But they are also responsible for what is best about the culture. Perhaps a good metaphor for all these Korean traits—wrath, Confucian principles, and nature fetishism—is its famously pungent cuisine. Or, as one Korean American chef described his food, "aggressive."

# 5

# KIMCHI AND THE CABBAGE
# INFERIORITY COMPLEX

• • • • • • • • • • • • • • • •

THERE ARE NOW SEVERAL MICHELIN STAR KOREAN
restaurants in the United States. This may come as a shock
to diasporic Koreans; many of us still bear the childhood
scars brought on by our non-Korean friends opening our
fridge for a snack and being repulsed by the smell of Korea's
national dish, the fermented spicy cabbage called kimchi.

And it's not a shame restricted to children; a Korean doctor I know who worked at a prominent Boston hospital early
in his career was told by his boss that the nurses were complaining of his breath. His wife changed her kimchi recipe to
include less garlic.

Being Korean in America when I was a child was like being a smoker now. We were pariahs with filthy smelly habits
that made our friends not want to come over to play.

Bobby Kwak, a successful entrepreneur based in New
York, is all too familiar with this scenario. Today, he is a
posterboy for Korean American cool. He is a hip restaurateur,

inventor of the prize-winning *bibimbap* (marinated beef barbecue, vegetables, and a fried egg burger), and owner of Circle—one of New York's hottest nightclubs, catering to high-rolling Koreans. But he recalls that not long ago being Korean was not cool in America. In his swank midtown Manhattan office, I asked him about what it was like growing up as a Korean American in northern New Jersey in the 1970s and 1980s. "It was embarrassing," he said, shielding his face with his hands.

He recalls that a large part of the shame came from the food. "One time when I was in third grade, my mom packed *jja jang myun*"—noodles with black bean sauce—"and *kkakdugi*"—pickled radish—"and put it in a thermos. My teacher made me dump it because the kids were all like, "'Who farted?'" So I had to tie it up in a plastic bag and take it outside. I was the only Asian American in my school at the time."

I hated Korean food as a child. My nanny was an American of Hungarian descent; she raised me on spaghetti and meatballs, mac and cheese, and stuffed cabbage. When my family moved to Korea, one of the biggest shocks for me was having to eat Korean food every day. The food was too spicy, and there were too many vegetables, some of them tough stems and roots that I was sure weren't edible, and chewing them made me feel like a cow.

My first winter in Korea, I saw something I'd never seen before: a *kimjang*—the nationwide custom of making enough kimchi to last the winter. This seemed to me like the lamest seasonal ritual ever. The Iranians have their annual rose festival in May, when the entire country celebrates roses and turns them into fragrant rosewater for food and for perfume. In New England, autumn means going apple picking and turning the harvest into pies, apple butter, and cider. In Germany, September and October means beer. Yet in Korea, the whole nation's autumnal agricultural ritual involves cabbage. Every household, rich or poor, takes dozens, scores, even hundreds of heads of Napa cabbage, and piles them into large rubber vats (the same kind in which many women washed their clothes) or, in many cases, the bathtub. Every individual leaf of every head of cabbage has to be massaged individually with a mixture of red pepper, salt, garlic, and fermented anchovy paste. To me this makes about as much sense as making sure there were enough cow pies to last the winter.

From an early age, I found *kimjang* absurd and irrational, which of course it wasn't. The fermentation process gave kimchi a long shelf life, enabling Koreans to eat vegetables all winter long and avoid vitamin deficiencies. Regardless of its origins, however, witnessing this ritual made me feel like Gulliver in all those strange lands with their incomprehensible customs. Gulliver arrives in new land and discovers acrid smell; finds whole country massaging cabbages; concludes they are doing it in service to the Wicker Man. Surely there must be a human sacrifice involved because such a society could not be sane. I simply did not see the payoff. Especially since I developed an anchovy allergy later in life, which meant I couldn't eat kimchi even if I wanted to.

Japan enjoys kimchi and has imported it by the ton for decades; they also make a less spicy version, called *kimuchi*. But historically, the Japanese nonetheless viewed kimchi as a sign of Korean peasant primitiveness. We were cabbage eaters, like the Irish. We delighted in the cheapest vegetable.

The issue came up last year when I was renting out my Paris apartment to a prospective tenant, a young student from Japan. As she only spoke Japanese, she had brought an interpreter, as well as a clueless French real estate agent who declared that it was a perfect fit of landlord and renter, because I was Korean and the renter was Japanese. The agent had no idea that she was dealing with inter-Asian tribalism—that the young woman and I were silently growling at each other like dogs, totally involuntarily. She opened the fridge and turned up her nose, saying something in Japanese to her interpreter. The latter told me, "She wants to know if you can get rid of the kimchi smell."

I said, "Please tell her I'm allergic to kimchi, I don't keep it in my fridge, and THAT IS THE SMELL OF FRENCH CHEESE." *Good luck living in this country*, I thought to myself.

Where was I? Yes, inter-Asian tribalism aside, in the 1990s, other countries—both Asian and non-Asian—began developing a taste for kimchi and started to import it. TH Lee, president of GSA Public Relations and Korean culture guru, explains: "In the 1990s, there was a wave of people seeking healthy cuisine. They discovered that Korean food was healthy. That was the beginning of the boom."

Lee Charm gives some insight into the philosophy underpinning Korean food. "Confucianism made its way into every aspect of life—even food. Food is based on the theory of the yin and yang, and the five elements. Every meal has to have five tastes: sour, bitter, sweet, spicy, and salty. There are also supposed to be five colors and five textures. Every housewife, without thinking of it, follows these rules. That's why Korean food is so healthy. It's based on the philosophy of the cosmic energy."

Many people outside Korea subscribe to the belief that Korean food contains mystic healing properties. The SARS bird flu epidemic of 2003 made kimchi ubiquitous throughout Asia. SARs raged throughout China, Southeast Asia, and even Canada and parts of Europe, with about 8,000 reported cases and about 750 deaths. Meanwhile, South Korea experienced zero bird flu–related deaths (there were two cases, both nonfatal). Many theories as to South Korea's immunity have been postulated; none were conclusive. One study suggested that the enzymes contained in kimchi strengthened immunity in birds; some people made the mental leap to assume that this also protected them from bird flu.

Through a combination of South Korea's own reports, a post hoc fallacy, and urban legend, China and other Asian countries concluded that kimchi was the magic elixir protecting the Koreans from the disease. In 2003, Korean kimchi exports went up 40 percent over the previous year; in China alone, the increase was 245 percent.[1]

Despite the preponderance of "evidence," I remained unconvinced about kimchi's medicinal benifits, so I consulted Jia Choi, who holds a PhD in Korean food from Ewha Womans University in Seoul. Choi is the president of Seoul-based O'ngo Food Communications.

I asked Choi why Koreans needed to eat something as extreme-tasting as kimchi, whose sodium, spiciness, and sourness literally draw the moisture from one's mouth. She explained that it had to do with compensating for the neutrality of rice. "In other countries, fish or meat is the staple," she said. "In Korea, it's rice. And kimchi goes really well with rice." Choi elaborated that all fermented items are highly addictive, not just kimchi. "It's the same with cheese and beer. When people start eating fermented items, it's hard for them to stop."

The Korean hot pepper used in kimchi is actually from Japan, which got it from Spain, which got it from the Americas. The pepper has only been in Korea since the seventeenth century. But the Japanese don't use the pepper. It leapfrogged over to Korea.

At first, said Choi, Koreans thought the hot chili pepper was inedible. Kimchi existed before that, but it was cured using salt alone. However, "salt was very expensive. In the 1750s, in order to reduce salt consumption, the government recommended using red pepper flakes, because this allows you to reduce the amount of sodium you use." Even back then the Korean government had a hand in micromanaging such matters as its citizens' diet.

Which is a trend that continues today. According to Choi, the popularity of kimchi spiked significantly after 2008; she believes this may have something to do with a campaign by former South Korean president Lee Myung-bak to raise global awareness of *hansik*, Korean food. His wife, Kim Yoon-ok, headed the government-funded Hansik Global Association, known abroad as the Korean Food Foundation.

Well, at this point, I'd have been surprised if the government *didn't* use its funds to promote Korean cuisine.

I went on a Seoul street food tour offered by Choi's company, O'ngo; it was a delight. There I found even more evidence of the Korean government spending public funds to promote Korean cuisine.

The tour group included Mike Traud, an associate professor at Drexel University in Philadelphia, where he teaches hospitality law in the culinary arts department. Traud had been taking a one-month cooking class at O'ngo because Drexel was planning to offer a semester-long course in Korean cuisine. This was unexpected, especially since, as he told me, the curriculum only offers three other nationally specific cuisines: French, Italian, and Chinese.

So why does Korean food have the good fortune to be singled out? The answer should not have surprised me, but it did: "We've been lucky to have the Korean government sponsor classes in the past. Three years ago, they brought ten students and two professors [to Korea] to understand Korean cuisine and cooking and bring it back to the States."

Even with government assistance, though, it's hard to convince people to try a new cuisine. So I asked him to explain the recent popularity of Korean food.

"In the United States," he said, "it stems from David Chang; he's the first one to make really mainstream Americanized Korean food. After Chang, you started to see his influence in menus. . . . People are experimenting with kimchi, pickles, fried chicken. Korean ingredients are being incorporated into various cuisines." The sudden popularity of Korean

taco trucks in major U.S. cities—particularly Los Angeles—
have helped popularize Korean flavors even in neighbor-
hoods without a Korean community.

David Chang—who used to be a junior professional
golfer—is one of the world's most famous chefs; with two Michelin stars, he is the pride and glory of the Korean American
foodie community. While most people can't afford to eat at his
New York restaurants Momofuku and Momofuku Ko, food
trends in the United States start with gourmands and review-
ers and trickle down to influence the tastes of the masses.

Full disclosure: the particular O'ngo tour I was on was
technically a drinking tour. Koreans drink *a lot*—in higher
quantities than such booze stalwarts as United States, UK,
France, Germany, or even Japan, according to the World
Health Organization.[2] The pastime of drinking has many
rituals. A night of drinking in Korea happens in upwards of
three different drinking establishments, in three phases. It's
not considered sporting to go home until everyone does.

The staples of a Korean bar crawl are beer and *soju*—a
potato wine cheaper than most types of bottled water. It's
sweet and goes down easily, so it's easy to overdo it, and it really packs one wallop of a hangover. Jinro Soju is the most
popular brand; astonishingly, it is also the world's number-
one-selling liquor brand, surpassing the likes of Smirnoff
vodka, Bacardi rum, and Johnnie Walker scotch. In 2012,
Jinro sold over 580 million liters worldwide.[3]

Even when you're totally plastered, you have to observe
basic Korean boozing etiquette: You don't pour your own al-

cohol; if you want some more, you hint at this by pouring alcohol into someone else's glass, whether this person wants it or not. That person must then offer to pour some into your glass. This is one of the reasons why there's so much peer pressure among Korean drinkers: if everyone around you has stopped drinking, you might have to wait for quite a while before someone offers to top off your glass.

A second and very important rule is that when you are pouring alcohol for someone, you pour with your right hand and use your left hand to hold your sleeve. My tour guide, Daniel Gray, explained that there are two reasons for this: in the old days, sleeves were big and billowy, so holding the sleeve closed was a way of keeping it out of the other person's drink; and by having both hands in plain sight, you are proving that you are not holding a knife.

Koreans know a lot of drinking games. Gray showed me one I hadn't seen before. "This one is called 'Titanic,'" he said. "It was taught to me by the very smart students at Yonsei University, who have no livers. It's kind of like Jenga but with beer." Basically, you're making a boilermaker very slowly. There are over a hundred different kinds of boilermakers—*poktanju*—in Korea. You put an empty shot glass in a large glass of beer, and everyone takes turns pouring *soju* into the shot glass. Whoever makes the shot glass sink has to drink the whole mixture.

Gray explained why *soju*, which is kind of rough on an empty stomach, was the perfect accompaniment to Korean food: "It's good at cutting the grease of the food," he said. "In fact, it's so good at cutting grease that they put it in spray bottles to clean the tables."

Hooni Kim, a renowned Korean American chef, owns two restaurants in New York: Danji (which has a Michelin star) and the brand-new Hanjan. He was in his third year of medical school and planning to specialize in neurosurgery when he decided to become a chef. Yes, his mother was very upset. "My mom didn't speak to me for almost a year," he said.

They've long since made amends, but now there's a new group of people who are almost as upset: Koreans who come to dine at one of his restaurants for the first time and discover that he charges for kimchi. It's downright revolutionary. From the point of view of Korean patrons, that would be like charging for tap water. He said proudly, "This is the only restaurant in New York that charges for kimchi. We don't charge a lot, but if it's free, people don't eat it. If it's free, we can't make it well. I'm a businessman. How can I focus on something that isn't generating revenue? If kimchi were free, it would always be the last focus, where it should be the first focus because it's our national dish." It's hard to argue with that logic.

Kim has a kind but warrior-like demeanor and a commanding presence. His staff clearly adore, fear, and respect him. I met him at Hanjan (Korean for "one glass"), and when he exited the kitchen and entered the restaurant area where I was sitting, the staff—none of them Korean—seemed excited to see him.

Kim told me about his unique path from the surgical scalpel to the chef's knife. He had intended just to take a year off between his third and fourth years of medical school. On a lark, he enrolled in classes at the International Culinary Center (formerly the French Culinary Institute) in New York. He offered to work as an unpaid intern at Daniel, New York's celebrated three-star Michelin restaurant of French chef Daniel Boulud.

Whatever he did during those two weeks impressed his bosses enough for them to offer him a full-time job. "I pretended to think about it, but as soon as I heard that, that was it, I was not going back to medical school."

It's hard to imagine a better training for a chef than the kitchen at Daniel. "I learned to cook the French way," he said. "It's the only way to cook. It is the right way to cook. It's the philosophy and principle that there are no shortcuts. There are, but in the end product, you'll see there is a difference. So do everything the right way." Then he said with an oratorical cadence that really reminded me of a French chef, "The right way is always longer. The right way always costs more money. The right way is just more difficult. But the food doesn't lie. People can really tell."

He went right to the third rail of Asian cooking: MSG—monosodium glutamate, a controversial food additive that supposedly enhances flavor. "For me, MSG is a shortcut. It's cheating. It's like athletes taking steroids. They're chemically trying to withdraw more flavor where there isn't any."

Of course, the proof of the pudding is in the eating, and the dishes I sampled were a revelation. I tried his *dukbokki*, which is a spicy rice cake snack that Korean schoolchildren often get when they're hanging out after classes. It's a comfort food, almost a junk food. But not the way Kim makes it. He cooks his in pork fat and garnishes it with tiny slivers of pepper that resemble saffron.

Hanjan's decor is chic, cozy, and modern, with very little in common architecturally with most of New York's other Korean restaurants. But Kim resists typifying his restaurant as an upscale one. "I still don't think Korean food is fine dining," he said, which made me raise my eyebrows. "The best food in France is cooked by the three-star Michelin chefs." By contrast, "I think the best food in Korea is cooked by the mothers and grandmothers. There is a history of restaurants in certain countries. Korea doesn't have that. Korean dining food history is *jumak*—home-cooking, casual street food, market food."

Surprisingly, Kim says his mother never cooked at home, noting that chefs usually fall into extremes in that regard: either they were inspired by their mother's cooking or they were forced to learn to cook because their mothers didn't. In Kim's case, the cold stove at home encouraged him to go out to eat with his friends. "I fell in love with the restaurant scene—the atmosphere, energy."

Another detail to which Kim pays fastidious attention is garlic; he says almost all the garlic out there is useless for his purposes. "Ninety percent of the garlic used in restaurants is from China," he said. "The flavor profile is that it's really powerful for the first four hours, but if you look at it as a graph, the line goes down. The next day you don't taste it anymore."

Kim is pleased at the global Hallyu phenomenon, but he doesn't think that food has a place in Hallyu. "For me food is so much more real than a pop song or a video," he said. As with all great chefs I've met, he talks about food as a man would talk about a woman he's in love with. Once more adopting his lyric speech rhythms, he said, "Looking, hearing is one thing. Tasting, touching is another. Smelling and tasting is the heart and soul of what Korea is. As much as pop culture wants to globalize, food is the best way for Koreans to share their soul and culture."

Turning the expression "you are who you eat" on its head, Kim said, "No. You eat who you are. No one describes who you are like your food."

# 6

# WHY POP CULTURE? OR, FAILURE IS THE BREAKFAST OF CHAMPIONS

• • • • • • • • • • • • • •

WHY WOULD KOREA FOCUS ON POP CULTURE AS A path to international success, one might well wonder, when this area has been the near-exclusive domain of the English-speaking world for a century? Korea's most influential popular culture critic, Lee Moon-won, pointed out, "Very few countries have ever attempted to sell their pop culture to the United States. Even Japan didn't try."

Korea's cultural ambitions are not just chutzpah. Nor did they come out of nowhere. They were born of necessity. And by necessity, I mean shame. After decades of concerted effort to pull itself out of poverty, South Korea's economic boom hit a wall in 1997 in the form of the Asian financial crisis.

If it were not for the crisis, there might never have been a Korean Wave. The debt emergency, which effectively halted many exports, forced South Korean industries—including entertainment—to think outside the box in order to make up for lost revenues.

Prior to the crisis, the South Korean entertainment industry didn't make an aggressive effort to peddle its wares overseas. After all, who the hell wants to hear songs or watch shows in Korean? But with their backs to the wall, people in the entertainment industry decided that they had to sell their films, television shows, and music to the rest of Asia. Little did they know that they were planting the seeds for a regional addiction.

The financial crisis—which started in Thailand and was caused by a perfect storm of bad debt, lender panic, and regional contagion—affected most of Asia, including South Korea. In December 1997, the Korean government negotiated a loan of up to $57 billion from the International Monetary Fund. (They ended up using only $19.5 billion.) The day they made the loan request was called the Day of National Humility. President Kim Young-sam told his country via television that he was "whipping himself every day" in shame at having brought his country to this situation.

To this day, Koreans refer to the Asian financial crisis as the "IMF crisis"—because in their eyes, having to take out a loan was the unkindest cut of all. Amazingly, South Korea was able to pay back the loan in 2001—fully three years ahead of schedule. It's an achievement that economists today often refer to when discussing solutions to Europe's current debt crisis (ahem, Greece). How did South Korea do it?

Mostly, it was via draconian measures, such as putting a halt to loans that banks were giving all too freely to chaebols—

Korea's mega conglomerates like Samsung and Hyundai. This forced over half of South Korea's chaebols to shut down and led to painful side effects, including huge unemployment and increased interest rates.

Wealthy women relinquished their wedding rings and athletes turned in trophies and medals to be melted down into ingots to help the national cause. The gold drive raised some eight metric tons of privately donated gold in its first week alone.[1] South Korea knew that it was a poor country not long ago, and they had learned that defeating poverty was a national effort.

Paying back the loan was trivial compared to the larger underlying issue: Korea now had a serious image problem. TH Lee remembers getting an odd phone call from the Blue House—Korea's presidential residence and office—in February 1998. Incoming President Kim Dae-jung, who had the task of cleaning up the mess from the debt crisis, was asking Lee for his help. At the time, Lee was the head of the Korean branch of the global public relations giant, Edelman. "I thought, why would they want to call me? I'm a PR guy."

But that's exactly why they called Lee. Korea wanted to rebrand itself, quite possibly the biggest national rebranding campaign in world history. "They told me, 'Everyone believes Korea is in crisis and we are losing investors and a lot more.'" Hence the unprecedented move of a Korean president calling on a PR firm. It was a huge first step in what Lee describes as Korea's campaign to broadcast the message that it was "joining the global village."

Lee's approach was radical and Don Draperesque, in a

country that at the time had no Mad Men: If people think Korea is a country in crisis, why not spin it exactly that way? "Koreans are good at engaging in crisis," he said, pointing to all the times the country had been invaded—by Britain, Russia, China, Japan, and the United States. "Only two countries are still alive after hundreds of invasions: Scotland and Korea."

Thus, rather than hiding from the word "crisis," it in fact became the core message of a book he and then-president Kim Dae-jung published within a month of that Blue House call. The book—bearing the unambiguous title of *Korea: On Course and Open for Business*—was aimed at potential international investors. It focused on the notion that crisis brought out the best in people. It featured uplifting stories of Korean workers who were laid off and reinvented their lives by learning new skills. "Before the crisis, Korea was a closed country," said Lee. "Korean media saw international investors as the enemy, as an economic invader; but they opened their gates to the world."

Another huge shift was that Korean youth felt emboldened to be entrepreneurs. "Before the crisis, students were students," said Lee. "After the crisis, a lot of young people started businesses." He cites the example of Lee Jae-woong, the founder of Daum Communications, the company that created one of the world's first user-generated web portals. When Lee first started the company in 1995, he was fresh out of graduate school. But when the crisis hit Korea, he faced a choice: fold—or do something crazy. He went for crazy. TH Lee explained, "He sold company stock on the street. He said if you buy our shares, we'll buy you a winter coat. That was a crisis situation. Now he is a very rich man." In 2012, Daum earned about half a billion dollars in revenue.

The chaebols that did survive the crisis had to completely rethink their strategies. Samsung stopped making cars (good idea!) and focused on electronics; Hyundai did the reverse, scaling back its electronics division to focus on cars.

Korea made some of its best decisions in the wake of the crisis. Its information technology, pop, drama, film, and video game industries as we know them today all arose out of a last-chance, long-shot gamble to get out of this hole. (All these industries will be discussed in later chapters.)

A period of massive debt might seem like the worst time to try to build brand-new industries. Korea could coast on its already successful products, like mobile phones and semiconductors. Why would it want to shift its focus to something so intangible and fickle as the content industries, like pop culture?

This seemingly quixotic plan was the brainchild of President Kim Dae-jung. Kim was best known for his historic summit in 2000 with North Korean leader Kim Jong-il, and a photo of the two men shaking hands was a shot heard round the world. That year, Kim was awarded the Nobel Peace Prize. His final years (he died in 2009) were overshadowed by shocking allegations that he had essentially paid for the photo op, funneling hundreds of millions of dollars to the North Korean government. But as far as this book is concerned, Kim is the hero of Hallyu.

The IMF crisis had revealed a fault line in the Korean economy: the nation had become overly reliant on the chaebols—the mega conglomerates. This meant that if the chaebols fell, so fell the nation.

Korea has no natural resources and very little arable land. Compounding the problem is that labor costs have risen so dramatically in the last twenty years that the country cannot rely solely on manufacturing as a source of wealth.

Korea is held back by an additional political handicap. According to a Korean economist who is also my dad, Korea is lacking in one huge technological advantage from which nearly every other industrialized nation has benefited for years: the option of letting the military lead the technological curve. "Since World War II," he said, "countries have been investing heavily in technology for military and defense, and the research they produced trickles down to the private sector."

For example, the GPS technology that is now commonplace in smartphones and cars was first developed by the United States and the former Soviet Union in the 1970s for use in air force navigation and tracking nuclear warheads; jet engines were invented by Germany and the UK for use in World War II aircrafts.

By contrast, Korea is not permitted to pursue military technology on an aggressive scale. In accordance with the 1953 mutual defense treaty between South Korea and the United States, South Korea cannot make any major military decisions without U.S. support. In other words, Korea can't compete with the big technological players in certain areas. Thus it has been forced to focus elsewhere.

President Kim Dae-jung pushed information technology,

which was an obvious and easy point of entry: all you really need are coders. He also set his sights on popular culture.

According to Choi Bokeun, an official at Korea's Ministry of Culture, Sport, and Tourism, Kim marveled at how much revenue the United States brought in from films, and the UK from stage musicals. He decided to use those two countries as benchmarks for creating a pop culture industry for Korea.

Was Kim out of his mind? Building a pop culture export industry from scratch during a financial crisis seems like bringing a Frisbee instead of food to a desert island. But there was method to the madness. The creation of pop culture doesn't require a massive infrastructure; all that is required is time and talent. And countries have always exported goods that no one really needs. Did nineteenth-century China need Britain's opium? Did judges in Bombay need heavy, sweaty English barrister wigs? Did Korea need Spam?

The American in me understands how easy it is to take pop music for granted as something that moody teenagers listen to in order to piss off their parents or deal with the boredom of living in suburbia. But in places without a long history of liberalism—that is, much of the world outside the United States and western Europe—people have a direct, overwhelming connection to American pop music.

Pop culture—specifically, American pop culture—played a large role in the fall of communism. In 1989, the former Czechoslovakia's Velvet Revolution—in which the Communist regime was toppled in favor of a parliamentary democracy—was partly inspired by students listening to an American band, the Velvet Underground.

American pop culture was—for a time—the symbol of liberation for South Korea: American GIs introduced South Koreans to rock 'n' roll, Spam, and baseball—all of which became immensely popular and synonymous with freedom: freedom from the Japanese, freedom from communism. (Koreans still like Spam. A lot. Outside the United States, South Korea is the world's highest consumer of Spam.)

And now, it's Korea's turn. Korea looked to pop culture as a way to create new sources of revenue, unite people, and generate an exportable product that would help spread Korean culture globally.

K-culture has the potential to be a powerful diplomatic tool. I'm convinced that the late Korean president Kim Daejung will be proven right in his prediction that Hallyu, not politics, will bring north and south together.

North Korean black marketers are literally risking their lives to smuggle in copies of South Korean videos and dramas. In 2009, a North Korean defector to the south told *Time* magazine that in North Korea, bootleg American movies fetched 35 cents on the black market, whereas South Korean movies cost $3.75, because the punishment for being caught with the latter is much more severe.[2]

## THE WORLD'S COOLEST MINISTRY OF CULTURE

For the longest time, I couldn't hear the words "Ministry of Culture" without thinking of some horrible totalitarian state.

I was always reminded of the Ministry of Truth in George Orwell's dystopian novel *1984*, which produced lowbrow entertainment for the proletariat, such as insalubrious pulp novels written from a formula based on six mix-and-match plots.

I took a pretty dim view of the whole notion. That is, until I visited the Korean Ministry of Culture.

Imagine the top levels of government working on virtual reality and hyperrealistic hologram technology—but not for the purpose of warfare or espionage; rather, to make a mind-blowing concert experience. That's one of the projects undertaken by the Ministry of Culture, Sport, and Tourism.

What's so great about holograms? "Holograms are very important for the performing arts," said Choi Bokeun, who has the coolest title ever: director of the Popular Culture Industry Division. The explanation was not one I was expecting to hear from a bespectacled, gray-suited, highly educated official in the Korean central government.

Primarily, his focus is on Korean pop music, fashion, mass entertainment, comic books, and web cartoons. Sounds like a party! But Choi has what I suspect is one of the most stressful jobs in contemporary Korea.

You would never guess from the building's imposing, high-ceilinged architecture and its dead-quiet corridors that any vaguely show-biz-related activity was taking place inside. Its atmosphere and employees were redolent of the Einstein Lab at Princeton.

One of Choi's division's roles is to promote the research and development of highly advanced "cultural technology."

I'd never heard that term before, but according to Choi, Hallyu depends on it and the government invests a great deal on it.

Holograms can enhance stage performances. For example, a K-pop band can give a quasi-live simultaneous performance in all the world's major cities without actually being physically present.

Also in the works are artificial rainbows, as well as fireworks whose shapes can be manipulated and changed at will—for example, to take the shape of traditional Korean designs—without the use of CGI. "It's very tricky, but we're developing it," said Choi.

These technological feats are developed in cooperation with ETRI—Electronics and Telecommunications Research Institute—a Korean think tank and technology lab in the southern city of Daejon. They also work with the Korean Culture Technology Institute, a research and development laboratory dedicated to Korean culture technology, based in the southwestern province of Gwangju. Both are government-owned. Yeah. The Korean government owns the local equivalent of Industrial Light and Magic.

That said, Choi disagreed with my characterization that the government was the invisible hand behind Hallyu: "The Korean Wave is not guided by the Korean government; we just serve a coordinating function."

Pop culture is such a high priority for President Park Geun-hye that, shortly after taking office in early 2013, she upgraded Choi's team from a small task force to an entire division. Many other countries have government arts funding, but how many governments finance popular culture—or create a $1 billion investment fund to nurture it?

The ministry has three other cultural content industry divisions: one for video games, one for television, and one for cultural industry policy. Collectively, they are called the Cultural Content Office. Choi explained their role: "To create an ecosystem for all creators to play in a fair manner, with fair compensation. [We are] the rule setters." The cultural content divisions' most important role is protecting intellectual property and prosecuting copyright infringers. The ministry develops policies to penalize illegal file sharing of music, shows, movies, and published material; violators can be stripped of Internet service for six months. Every time someone sings a song in a *noraebang*, or karaoke room, the artist is supposed to receive royalties. Choi's division writes those policies.

After the Asian financial crisis, President Kim Dae-jung created a special fund to create the Cultural Content Office. The initial annual budget was $50 million; now, said Choi, it's around $500 million. Choi's own budget is 10 percent of that total budget, or $50 million. Choi said the Cultural Content Office is now the "nucleus" of Korea's soft-power strategy.

Naturally, budget management and fund disbursement is a day-to-day part of the job. The Cultural Content Office has two budget controls. One is spending on cultural projects: for Choi, that comes out of his $50 million annual budget. But that's not even close to being enough money to achieve Korea's pop cultural ambitions.

Hence the second means of funding for the Korean culture machine: an investment fund—not to give free grants, but a for-profit fund, very much aimed at making high returns. Currently the fund size is a staggering $1 billion. That entire fund is earmarked just for the Korean pop culture industry; it does not include the fine arts like museums, opera, or ballet. (Those industries are run by an entirely separate division. Koreans take culture very seriously.)

According to Choi, about 20 to 30 percent of the fund comes from the Korean government; the rest of the monies are from investment banks and private companies, such as music labels. This fund is, in turn, operated by the Korean Venture Investment Corporation (KVIC), made up of private-sector fund managers. "The fund invests mostly in film," said Choi, "but also in animation, music, and drama."

Unsurprisingly, the cultural content industry divisions have a five-year plan: their aim, said Choi, is for the market size of the collective Korean cultural industry exports to reach $10 billion—more than double the current figure. That's a tall order.

The Ministry of Culture oversees projects on a level of detail you could not imagine: for example, regulating Korea's many *noraebangs*. Part of this is vice control: "We want a 'singing room' to have a family-friendly environment where people can enjoy singing clean songs," Choi explained.

To that end, the *noraebangs* are legally classified into three types: One type is not permitted to sell alcohol, but some owners sell it illegally anyway, so the government tries to monitor this. The second kind is allowed to sell alcohol. And the third kind, said Choi, blushing as he did so, "is the one where you can be with women." The Koreans call the third type a "room salon." Choi's ministry only concerns itself with the first kind of *noraebang*; the latter two are regulated by the police bureau and the Ministry of Welfare and Health. Who knew that karaoke rooms required so much bureaucratic hassle and such a staggeringly complex taxonomy? For that matter, who knew that karaoke rooms were such a popular hooker hangout?

The government is also raising private funds to build Hallyu World, a multicomplex theme park, in Ilsan, a town northwest of Seoul. Hallyu World will include a private fifteen-hundred-seat concert hall, as well as hotels and a K-culture-themed shopping area. The scale of investment is $200 million, with a projected finish date of 2016.

I asked Choi whether he thought Hallyu was a passing fancy. His answer was characteristically pragmatic: "No, because there are so many investors." It's true; if people throw money at something, it tends to stay alive. He also reiterated that the government's role was merely that of coordination. The future of Hallyu, he said, is "all up to the Korean people, the private sector. It's not up to the Korean government."

Inevitably, though, certain aspects of Hallyu don't reap the benefits of government promotion. One person who feels left in the cold is Kim Heon-jun, the head of Jinjo Crew— Korea's most successful B-boy (street dancing or break-dancing) troupe. As with most young Korean celebrities, his rebellious exterior belies an exceptional politeness. He's dressed to look tough, yet he uses the most respectful form of

Korean address with me, except on a few occasions when he good-naturedly called me a *seh-ggi* (meaning "bastard," but not as strong).

I met with him in the empty, echoing lobby café of the Chungmu Art Hall in Seoul; he was there for a rehearsal, but he could not have looked more out of place in the buttoned-down theater and gallery space. His manner of dress is what counts for hopelessly rebellious in Korea: a black baseball cap turned backwards, a casual T-shirt, and black nylon track pants. Kim looks and behaves a decade younger than his twenty-seven years, and on a bathroom break he sprinted. "There's no need to rush!" I said. He replied, "I run everywhere. Walking is a waste of time, right?"

Kim has led Jinjo Crew to several first-place victories in world B-boy tournaments, but he feels his sport is not getting the attention it deserves—he feels overshadowed by K-pop. When I mentioned to him that I was about to meet Choi for an interview, his face lit up and he said, "Really? Please make sure you tell him to help us."

"What exactly would you like me to say?" I asked.

"For real, B-boy is more famous internationally than K-pop, but I don't think [the government] realizes that. We're not just playing around. There's so much attention on K-pop but we're not just a fad; this is a culture. In other countries, B-boy culture is really huge, but in Korea we don't have any support from the government. Ask him to pay attention to B-boys too, or else we'll lose all our good dancers to other countries that care more about this art. Please."

I forgot to relay Kim's message. But my exchange with the street dancer is emblematic of the absurdity of modern Korea: in what other country would a B-boy try to make the case that he deserves his government's support?

# 7

# WHEN KOREA BANNED
# ROCK 'N' ROLL

· · · · · · · · · · · · · · ·

SAY WHAT YOU WILL ABOUT THE QUALITY OF K-POP music, but Lee Moon-won, Korea's most influential pop culture critic, made a shockingly frank pronouncement in describing K-pop: "Koreans are not good at creativity."

If he's right, then President Park Geun-hye's promise of turning Korea into a "creative economy" is in trouble.

Sitting across from him, my eyes widened and I asked him to elaborate. "Koreans are better at packaging and marketing. Look at Samsung, for example. With K-pop, the songwriters are not Korean. They're European. The people who do the editing studied in the United States; they're multinational. The dance choreographers are from everywhere. It's really a factory."

Many of the songwriters *are* European—Swedes especially. "Korean pop is based on Europop," Lee explained. Which totally explains why K-pop songs sound like Eurovision Song Contest entries. He elaborated, "The European sound influence is electronic and techno music. There's a heavy electronic base."

K-pop boy bands TVXQ! and Big Bang are examples of Europop-influenced acts; other K-pop bands fall into other mainstream genres like R & B (Rain or MBLAQ) or bubble gum pop (Girls' Generation).

There's a very good reason for the lack of an original, homegrown Korean sound: the Korean pop scene got a very late start because of censorship that stifled musical talent and creativity. For a critical period during the 1970s, rock music was banned in Korea.

As a consequence of this ban, the Korean pop sound did not absorb any influence from the whole 1970s sound progression, including classic rock, punk, glam rock, and early heavy metal. No Led Zeppelin, No Sex Pistols, no David Bowie.

During his eighteen-year rule from 1962 to 1979 (ending with his assassination), President Park Chung-hee (father of current South Korean President Park Geun-hye) instituted on-again, off-again martial law. Park was the hero behind Korea's rags-to-riches ascent (and—full disclosure—my grandfather's employer). It's now considered politically incorrect to refer to Park as a dictator, but I am failing to find another word to describe someone who amends voting laws to all but ensure his presidency for life.

Park's iron-fisted policies were partly in response to North Korea, which was putting most of its resources into building its military; this made South Korea extremely nervous. In 1972, Park responded to the threat of invasion as any sensible ruler would: by banning miniskirts, long hair on men, and rock 'n' roll. That pretty much ruled out mods, rockers, and hippies—imminent threats to national security.

Police would stop women on the streets, take a ruler to their skirts, and force them to go home and change if the gap between the hemline and the knee exceeded twenty centimeters. They would grab long-haired men and cut off their hair on the spot. No doubt these tactics will go down in the annals of history as the most effective war prevention gesture of all time. I'm sure that the North Korean rulers were quivering in their boots when they got wind of it.

Wi Tack-whan, head of the Korean Culture and Tourism Institute, recalled, "You couldn't have English words on your clothes or you'd get arrested. Even if you carried a guitar around, they would take it away. Songs were a way of protest."

I have to say, there are times when I feel I wouldn't object to an ordinance against excessive public guitar-playing. If you'd ever been to a Korean picnic, you'd understand. In the hands of an annoying person with no sense of self-awareness, a guitar is like a gun. At the school or multifamily picnics of my youth, someone—often, several people—would bring guitars. For some reason, Korea's favorite place to hold a picnic is on top of some mountain. I hate climbing and I hate the outdoors. So I would already be in a resentful mood, which would only worsen when these guys would whip out their guitars and make everyone sing Korean folk songs that I didn't know—and Koreans know lots and lots of songs. A guitar at a picnic signals you will not be going home for a very long time.

That's the basis of my guitar phobia. The late president

Park Chung-hee's guitar phobia must have been even more extreme, since he banned the songs of Bob Dylan, Joan Baez, and John Lennon's solo work, notably "Imagine."

A tragic victim of the bans was Korean psychedelic rocker Shin Joong-hyun, sometimes called the "Godfather of Korean Rock." Like pretty much every major Korean pop singer from the 1950s to the 1980s, Shin learned to love rock by listening to the American Forces Korea Network (AFKN) radio broadcasts. Shin's career began as a performer for the Eighth U.S. Army—the battalion that fought in the Korean War and remains stationed in Korea to this day, though in diminished numbers. Shin performed his first-ever concert at age nineteen at the Seoul army base in 1957.

Shin was probably the last experimental Korean pop musician to be known outside his home country. His 1970 cover of Iron Butterfly's "In A Gadda Da Vida," a live performance that can be seen on YouTube, is a revelation, sung with more vibrancy than the original.

In 1972, Shin was asked to write a song celebrating President Park's government. Shin, who opposed Park's dictatorship, refused. But that refusal cost him dearly. The government started to censor his songs, and in 1975 he was imprisoned on charges of marijuana possession. Shin said he was tortured and put into a psychiatric hospital. His works continued to be banned in Korea until Park's assassination in 1979.

But even when political oppression ceased to be an issue, Shin faced another obstacle altogether: in the absence of real rock influences, Korean pop music tastes had deteriorated.

Journalist Mark Russell wrote about Shin for his book, *Pop Goes Korea*:

"The rock trend passed by in the late 1970s to be replaced by a curious blend of disco, modern synthesizers, and a return to the old trot tunes that Park Chung-hee had enjoyed—it was the start of the bubblegum pop and syrupy ballads that have ruled Korea ever since. [Shin said,] "It was completely physical, with no spirit, no mentality, no humanity. That trend has carried over all the way to today, so people are deaf to real music. They don't know because they are never exposed to it."[1]

I feel for Shin. When my family moved to Korea in the mid-1980s, the music was of a type I have rarely heard before or since. It was nothing like current K-pop, and it wasn't like American pop either. The closest comparison would be to the French *chanson*, heartfelt songs of loss.

Musically, the songs were mostly in the minor key, which got to be depressing. And the singers had a habit of pseudo-operatic trilling in a way that you might hear from your untalented weirdo aunt when she's attempting to upstage everyone in an unnecessarily dramatic rendition of "Happy Birthday."

To be fair, there's a very good reason it took so long for Korea to find its musical niche, and it predates President Park Chung-hee's cultural crackdown. Korea had very little musical identity for much of the twentieth century. During the Japanese occupation from 1910 to 1945, the use of the Korean language was banned, and by default Koreans adopted Japanese cultural trends.

Following liberation from Japan, Korea had to build a

nation anew. It needed a national anthem. President Syng-man Rhee's regime chose a turn-of-the-century poem for the song's lyrics. As for the melody? "Auld Lang Syne," which must have made Korean New Year's Eve parties very confusing. Only later, in 1948, was the anthem set to original, Korean-composed music.

During the Korean War, musicians had only one audi-ence wealthy enough to keep them from starving: "From the 1950s to the 1980s, most Korean pop singers started out as entertainers for the U.S. Army," said Wi Tack-whan. "The pay was really good. And until 1972, there were sixty thou-sand soldiers—that's a huge military presence, and a lot of opportunity."

The USO took entertainment very seriously, featuring Hollywood stars like Marilyn Monroe. According to Wi, "The U.S. military hired Hollywood professionals to audition Ko-rean musicians, so it was very competitive."

One act that got its start at the U.S. Army bases in Seoul was the Kim Sisters—Aija, Mia, and Sue. Most people have not heard of this singing trio, but at their height in the 1950s and 1960s, they were almost as big a Vegas act as the Rat Pack. They appeared on *The Ed Sullivan Show* twenty-five times, ranking them among the top ten most frequent acts in the history of the show, which aired from 1948 to 1971.[2] They ap-peared more often than Louis Armstrong or Patti Page. In fact, they appeared on the *Sullivan* show as often as the very act on which they modeled themselves: the McGuire Sisters.

Imagine what Asian Americans must have felt in 1959, the first time the Kim Sisters appeared on the *Sullivan Show*.

I was incredulous even in 2013, watching their old clips on variety shows, being introduced by the likes of Dean Martin. In one clip, the Kim Sisters appear on a 1960s-era Saturday night variety show, *The Hollywood Palace*. The host opened with: "We have three sisters from Korea who rate among the most versatile entertainers in the business. They play about twenty instruments: saxophone, clarinet, trumpet, drums, and several others. They would have played more, but you know how kids are: they hated to practice!" Wow, what a knee-slapper. But how could the writers get away with a punch line containing no mention of race?

Then the three beaming, fair-complexioned, long-legged girls sang, "I Think I'm Going Out of My Head," a doo-wop hit originally performed by Little Anthony and the Imperials in 1964. They looked largely indistinguishable from any other girl group one might see on the show. Long, slinky, glittery dresses with a slit up the side, false eyelashes, and shiny, gigantic bouffant hairdos. It was the first time I'd ever seen Korean women dressed like that, and it was as jarring as a 1920s photo of a Korean flapper.

For their next number, they sang in Korean. I wouldn't be surprised if the Kim Sisters were the last musical group before Psy to sing a song entirely in Korean on American national television. The only bit of orientalism in that number was that they all whipped out fans and started flapping them daintily because . . . they were warm, I suppose.

Many African Americans speak about their shock the first time they saw Nichelle Nichols playing Uhura on the original *Star Trek* series. Actress Whoopi Goldberg recalled telling her family, "I just saw a black woman on television, and she ain't no maid."[3] That's how a generation of Korean Americans must have felt about the Kim Sisters.

I had the privilege of speaking with Sue (born Sook-ja), the eldest of the group, from her home in Las Vegas.

Perhaps no other pop cultural entity is a better symbol of South Korea's twentieth-century rags-to-riches story than the Kim Sisters. They are South Korea. Their mother started the band during the Korean War out of sheer survival mode: the family had lost their father and their home. Like almost every major Korean pop act through the 1980s, they got their start performing for American GIs stationed in Korea.

Before the war, the Kim parents were famous staples of the Korean entertainment world. At the beginning of the war in 1950, the North Koreans commandeered the family's house in Seoul and arrested their father. Sue witnessed it all. She was nine years old.

The reasons for the father's arrest are unclear. Sue recalls one of her mother's theories: "He was genius talented. They wanted to brainwash him and use him. And he wouldn't go for it."

During his lifetime, however, the girls' father inadvertently gave them a means of survival after he was gone. He taught them how to sing together in harmony by hitting them. "I can't believe he did that," recalled Sue. "Anyone who made a mistake would get smacked until we got red cheeks. He would not stop until we got it right."

Like Korea as a whole during and after the war, Sue's

mother had to improvise, and fast. She pulled together two of her seven children—daughters Sook-ja (to whom she gave the stage name Sue) and Aija. Then she recruited her niece Mia (née Minja.)

The sister act would later prove to be not just a show biz gimmick but a necessity: in order to get passports to go to the United States for their first performance, Mia could only accompany them if she was really their sister. So the mother legally adopted her and fudged Mia's birth date. "All the birth certificates had burned [in the war]," explained Sue.

Mrs. Kim started booking gigs for the Kim sisters to perform for the U.S. troops stationed throughout Korea. She decided on an American repertoire and "bought records on the black market," Sue recalled. The first song Mrs. Kim taught them was "Ole Buttermilk Sky," originally sung by Hoagy Carmichael in 1946.

The GIs loved the girls, dubbing them "the Korean McGuire Sisters." Sue said, "I think the soldiers were homesick. They appreciated three little Korean girls trying to entertain them. They would say, 'You should go to America, you'd make a lot of money.'"

Upon hearing that, the gears in Mrs. Kim's head started turning. "She didn't take it lightly," said Sue. And in fact, it turned out that the GI promises were not just hot air. In 1955, she said, "we got a call from one of the GIs saying he would go back to the United States and sign up the Kim Sisters and take them to America."

The girls' mother wasted no time in getting them ready for this possibility, even if it never materialized—a precursor to the modern-day K-pop training phenomenon, you might say. "She was playing a long shot," said Sue. "My mother knew that if we went to America, just singing was not enough to compete with other groups. Number one, the language barrier. So she said, you have to be different. You have to play a lot of instruments." Mrs. Kim also started the girls on ballet and tap-dancing lessons.

Mrs. Kim's long shot paid off. The GI grapevine reached entertainment producer Tom Ball, who flew to Korea in 1958 to check out the Kim Sisters. "The rest is history," said Sue. "He saw us, he liked us, we signed a contract."

But nothing in South Korea was easy in those years following the Korean War, when chaos and lost paperwork made departing the nation very complicated. The 1950 disappearance of Sue's father turned out to be an endless punishment: as if it weren't bad enough that he was gone, the Korean government cited the vagueness of his fate as a reason for denying them passports. According to Sue, "They said, 'We don't know if your father's alive; we can't give you a passport.'

"The South Korean government said that if the three girls go to America, they might go to North Korea"—the reasoning here being that the girls, if given the opportunity to leave the country, would try to find their father in the north. But after a year of Mrs. Kim "torturing herself" and relentlessly leveraging her celebrity to pursue every contact she had, the visa came through.

The girls were to be the closing act for a Vegas spectacular, Tom Ball's China Doll Revue, performed in the Thunderbird Hotel in 1959. A poster advertising the show promised "the most beautiful Oriental Show Girls in the World." After four weeks at the Thunderbird, they signed on to perform at the nearby Stardust Hotel for eight months. Ed Sullivan spotted them there and booked them for his show.

I asked Sue whether she experienced jeering or racist remarks from the audience. "You know, I'm glad you brought that up," she said. "My mother told me before we left, 'You might get some loud person in the audience, prejudiced. Or discrimination. Because in the Korean War, [Americans] lost their sons. They will blame you for it. This might happen.' But honestly, that never ever happened. When I hear about these black singers—Lena Horne, Nat King Cole, what they went through is amazing. How did they do it? But we never had that."

Sue's cousin Mia is now living in Hungary with her husband; Aija died of lung cancer in 1987. Sue retired from show biz in 1993 and lives in Las Vegas with her husband, John Bonifazio. The couple met in 1965 when the Kim Sisters were performing in a New York hotel. Bonifazio asked her out after attending their show seven nights in a row. The couple married in 1968; they have two children and five grandchildren. During my phone interview with Sue, John piped in with occasional background remarks to his wife, including, "You still have great legs."

Sue's journey from war-torn Korea to the Rat Pack–era Vegas Strip seems worlds away from Psy's career trajectory. But Sue, who loves Psy, sees a continuum between herself and him: "I told my son, now that Psy is this big, people are going to ask me, who were the first Koreans to come to America and make a name for themselves? Obviously [the Kim Sisters] name is going to come out."

# 8

# THE LEAN, MEAN, STAR-
# MAKING K-POP MACHINE

• • • • • • • • • • • • • • • •

THE K-POP STAR-MAKING PROCESS HAS SUFFERED many slings and arrows from the western press, including allegations that it is modern-day slavery. Yes, it's true that K-pop labels recruit budding child stars and bind them to ironclad contracts that can last as long as thirteen years. What you have to understand, though, is that Korea had no other way of building a pop industry.

President Park Chung-hee's aforementioned rock ban forced Korea to miss the British invasion, with the exception of the Beatles. In the 1960s, most of the world began to listen to rock bands that had formed on their own—without the help of a producer or record label Svengali. The British Invasion bands wrote their own songs and played their own instruments without a separate, anonymous backup band (country and jazz also had self-contained bands, but I'm talking strictly rock music). The Beatles began more or less as childhood friends from Liverpool—John Lennon met Paul McCartney in 1957 while performing at a dinky local celebration for the crowning of the Rose Queen. Paul then asked his friend George Harrison to join the band. They were all between fourteen and sixteen years old when they met. The Rolling Stones' front man, Mick Jagger, and songwriter Keith Richards were childhood friends in Kent.

This was never going to happen in Korea. Kids didn't have the free time to jam with friends or form bands. They were studying all the time. *All* the time. And if they weren't studying, it was likely because they were helping their parents run the family business. If Korea wanted a pop music industry, it was going to have to create it from the ground up. It didn't have time to wait around for four random geniuses (okay, three) to meet on their own on the streets of Liverpool or at some pub.

Why does it matter how a band gets formed?

It matters a great deal. The organically formed, self-contained bands had one crucial, history-altering characteristic: because they came from nothing, they had nothing to lose. They could experiment with new sounds; they could improvise. They could create musical revolutions. Koreans didn't have that. In the 1960s, Korea was a very poor country. Even a working-class Liverpudlian had a higher standard of living, and a hell of a lot more free time, than many monied Koreans did at the time.

Furthermore, there is one major difference in western versus Korean culture: western kids can goof off. In the unforgiving Confucian culture of Korea, however, a young person who screws up has a hard time getting back on track. There aren't really any second chances. Up until the last ten years or so, when K-pop started to prove hugely profitable, no Koreans would have risked their future to try to strike out on their own as a musician. If a Korean music industry was to form, it didn't have time to wait for the Korean John, Paul, George, and Ringo to magically find each other.

Malcolm Gladwell's bestselling book *Outliers* cites the Beatles as an example of the "10,000-hour rule," the theory that the difference between a brilliant achiever and one who is merely very good is that the former has invested at least 10,000 hours of practice in the craft. The Beatles, argued Gladwell, got in well over 10,000 hours between the McCartney-Lennon meeting in 1957 and their American debut in 1964, including 1,200 performances together as a band.

If it really takes 10,000 hours to make a great band, then the K-pop convention of the seven- to thirteen-year contract is entirely rational, especially since half that time is spent training the stars before they make any public appearances.

Shin Hyung-kwan, general manager of MNET, Korea's version of MTV, explained why the process takes so long. "It takes time to see who has hidden talents. It's one thing to pick some person and say you're going to make them a star, but you have to see if they get along with each other and in society at large. If you are not careful, the whole thing can be spoiled. Westerners do not understand. The performers could get into an accident, some kind of trouble."

Yet the K-pop contract remains controversial, not just in its duration but in its inflexibility. This was proven recently by a three-year legal battle between former king of the boy bands TVXQ! and its label, SM Entertainment; the issue was finally resolved at the end of 2012. The band members wanted out of their contract, citing long hours and rough working conditions. The label agreed to release TVXQ! from its contracts and in exchange, TVXQ! had to cease to exist. TVXQ! was dissolved in 2009, then the label reinstated it in 2010 with two of the five original members.

On the one hand, the stringent contracts are indeed part of Hallyu's success—the performers dance and sing well because they're recruited young and trained for years. On the other hand, the TVXQ! contract reveals that the band is paid shockingly poorly compared to top American bands. The artists don't get a guaranteed percentage of album sales until fifty thousand units have sold.[1]

If these K-pop aspirants had taken a traditional path, though, overwork would have been their fate anyway. "Of course we don't want people to be stuck in contracts, but these kids are so passionate," says Martina Stawski, a Canadian expat in Seoul who cohosts the popular video blog Eat Your Kimchi. "This is a big chance for them. They might work ridiculously hard at [becoming a pop star], but even if they join a chaebol they'll work ridiculously hard anyway. It's up to them to decide, 'Do I want to go to a *hakwon* every night till 1 am to slave away for a university entrance exam? Or, do I want to be a pop star?' "

"That's how the west sees all of Asia, not just K-pop," says culture critic Lee Moon-won. "They think we're all robots. We can't do anything about the fact that the west sees us that way. Koreans spend the same effort on everything, whether it's college entrance exams or an office job. Korea stands for hard work."

Lee offered additional insight as to why the K-pop star factory system is a necessity. "The U.S. population is 300 million, and Korea only has 50 million. Yet Korea has the same number of pop artists as the United States." In the United States, explained Lee, the pool of hopefuls wanting to be stars is big enough that natural triage occurs for stars to rise to the top.

Korean record labels don't have this luxury of waiting for stars to come to them. "The human resource pool in Korea is small," says Lee. "They have to take measures to be competitive internationally."

I interviewed Lee in his cramped Seoul office in the Yoido commercial district, out of which he runs a weekly watchdog magazine called *Media Watch*. He had a shaved head and facial stubble, and wore a white T-shirt. On the table before him, he had lined up a pack of cigarettes, his phone, and an ashtray neatly in a row and futzed with them as he spoke, periodically making slight adjustments in their placement. He reminded me of the old-school *Rolling Stone* journalists from the 1970s, back in the day when music writers thought of themselves as having a real social responsibility.

Lee observed that the job of critic is a very recent one in Korea. "When I was a kid, there was no [culture] criticism, but now that has changed. Korea has only been a democracy since 1987. Since then we have made significant advances. Korean politics is very fast."

According to Lee, his mighty pen has no influence on sales. "Fans don't care about reviews; they just buy music. MP3s are so cheap that it doesn't matter. [My reviews] don't have a huge effect from a business point of view. But if a musician has a bad reputation as an artist, it does affect whether they can get television appearances or radio play."

This points to a crucial difference between Korean and western culture. As Lee succinctly puts it: "There is no 'bad boy' model in Korea. Everyone is a *chak han* kid." A *chak han* kid is a good kid, with the implication of innocence. It's different from simply being "good." A philanthropist giving millions of dollars to a charity is performing a good deed, but it is not a *chak han* deed. A kid who helps his grandmother with the washing up is doing a *chak han* deed. It is on a smaller scale than goodness, and it refers more to conforming with traditional social values rather than spiritual or metaphysical goodness.

"Koreans position themselves as a good boy or good girl," he elaborated. "So if an artist is using drugs, then people get upset, so there is a big problem. [Something like this] can ruin a career, especially a sex scandal." Note, however, that on stage there is a lot of "sexiness" going around, like the female pop star Hyuna—but in her interviews and the way she conducts herself in the public eye, she is all sweetness and light.[2]

While the outright bans of the Park Chung-hee dictatorship exist no more, record labels and artists still have to reckon with the youth protection laws, which Korea instituted in the 1990s partly to clamp down on sexual exploitation of children and partly to protect children from material that might corrupt them. The latter category is open to interpretation.

In response to the laws, record labels assign strict age limits on albums, sometimes for odd reasons. "Mirotic," a song by boy band TVXQ!, could originally only be purchased by those over eighteen because of the lyrics "I've got you under my skin" (in English), which had to be changed to "I've got you under my sky" in order to be legally sold to a younger audience.

The penalties for being consigned to the nineteen+ age rating are high; it means the song in question gets no radio or TV play. When Lady Gaga's "Born This Way Ball" toured in Seoul, her concert was limited to the nineteen+ crowd with another turn of the screw: anyone eighteen and under was barred from entry *even if accompanied by an adult.*

Lee said of Korea's censorship laws, "The standards are very vague and inconsistently applied." One of the most puzzling bans—well, puzzling to an outsider but obvious to a Korean—was the ban on Japanese music, films, manga, and movies. Japanese bands were not permitted to do live concerts in Korea. The laws did not start to ease up until 1997—and even now, it has not been lifted entirely.

The loosening of the rules is shockingly slow and shockingly recent. In 1999, Korea started permitting Japanese films to be shown in theaters if, and only if, they had won prizes at international film festivals.

Lee's explanation for the Japanese ban was somewhat cynical, or pragmatic: despite the pretext that the ban was a response to Japan's erstwhile colonization of Korea, the real reason was pure business: the Korean government and culture industries were worried about the Japanese taking over the local market. Now, the quality of Korean cultural goods has improved, so Korea feels "less threatened," said Lee.

## THE CONGLOMERATE CASH COW

A staggering 4 percent of the population of South Korea auditioned in 2012 for *Superstar K*, Korea's biggest televised singing competition. That's 2.08 million would-be K-pop stars competing in a single year in a country with a population of 50 million. By contrast, even the behemoth *American Idol* only has about 80,000 contestants in a given year, amounting to a minuscule 0.03 percent of the U.S. population.

What this attests to is that the Hallyu Wave, and the Korean government's strategy to capitalize on it, has caused a tectonic shift in how young Koreans are viewing their future.

"Until about ten to fifteen years ago, [Koreans] didn't think of music and film as a legitimate business," said Shin Hyung-kwan, whose network, MNET, airs the *Superstar K* reality show. "Overseas, performers are called 'performing artists.' But here, we thought of them as *ddan ddara*"—meaning "hustler," a slang word possibly of Japanese origin. "We associated them with performers at gentleman's clubs. But now, as of two or three years ago, the most desired job is to be a singer." Shin is an emblem of the new respectable face of Korean entertainment: calm and educated, corporate with a bit of hip tweaking: high-fashion glasses and a well-pressed black Nehru-style jacket.

MNET, South Korea's most important music video channel, is owned by CJ E&M, Korea's largest entertainment group, a subsidiary of the CJ Group—an independent spinoff of Samsung. (Large Korean companies with an ounce of sense have their finger in the K-pop pie. As does the Korean government, which has invested heavily in K-pop.) CJ has an established fifteen-year-old brand for its music television network MNET, and its movie division is one of the most successful movie producers and distributors in Asia.

CJ and Samsung no longer have any ties, even though they are owned by members of the same family. But CJ E&M certainly has astounding business acumen reminiscent of its former parent company.

Speaking of the company, Shin said, "There is no equivalent in other countries." He's not kidding. CJ E&M is the quintessential Korean pop culture company in that it is made up of completely integrated units that all feed off each other in a highly efficient, highly profitable ecosystem. Its divisions include music television (such as MNET), film distribution, live entertainment (they staged *Mamma Mia* in China), video games, and "smart media," which is basically a social media web 2.0 platform for marketing all of the above. When CJ E&M puts on a concert, it also simultaneously releases a music video game and a dance video game related to the concert's theme. This sort of "one hand washes the other" model is what Korea has become known for.

The company was founded in 1995, but in 2011 it was spurred on to become the brand it is today by a desire to keep the competition from other Asian nations at bay. It is hard to imagine too many companies outside Korea that could pull off this kind of pan-entertainment model so rapidly. And if they did, it would take years for them to catch up.

How has success been achieved so quickly?

The CJ E&M ecosystem business model is a good example of Korea's general export strategy: it depends on a unanimous understanding that the whole is greater than the sum of its parts. The Korean government, its entertainment companies, IT companies, and even corporations that have nothing to do with entertainment know that they have to work together in order to pull off Hallyu world domination.

There is another, bleaker reason why Korea has little reason to fear that other countries will try to emulate the K-pop export model: the star-making process is so unpleasant that there are not many countries whose aspiring stars would put up with it. Korean youth, meanwhile, are used to intense sadomasochistic academic pressure, extreme discipline, constant criticism, and zero sleep.

Of course, there are other countries that have motivated, hardworking young people who would do anything to be stars. (India comes to mind.) But those countries, frankly, lack Korea's financial resources and organizational skills to turn these stars into world exports. The K-pop model re-

quires music companies to invest a lot of money up front for a
very distant return.

"K-pop is a five- to seven-year plan," comments Lee Moon-
won, "and the U.S. can't do that." In other countries, it would
not be profitable to put up so much money for training.

Many K-pop music executives may have entered the business thinking they were going to be managers of musicians,
but they found out that their role was really that of long-term
babysitter. K-pop is a paternalistic system that disciplines its
stars. This isn't just a matter of whether band members get
along; it's also necessary to steer them away from drunk driving, drugs, or sex scandals. K-pop star training is an education of the whole person. Which is also why band members
are taught etiquette.

I remember when K-pop started to become huge. It
seemed very abrupt. Korea had all this substandard sad music, and then in the mid-1990s it seemed to have derivative
music that was very slick, but not that different from the most
unimaginative incarnations of American rhythm and blues.
Then, seemingly out of nowhere, K-pop had become as cool
as it was unique, mesmerizing, exquisite, and habit-forming.

It seemed like a sudden and abrupt change, as if Korea
had suddenly decided to go off the metric system or drive on
the other side of the road. MNET, which launched in 1997,
was instrumental in changing the Korean public's view of the
entertainment industry. Just as MTV changed the way Americans thought of music, so MNET transformed the song-
based product into a video-based one.

Then in the early 2000s, down came Rain: a chiseled, sensuous R & B singer who broke the mold. Rain's videos were the first I saw that bore what came to be the K-pop stamp. Highly artistic direction, stylized sets, as if the video were taking place in the Matrix, and ingeniously choreographed.

Rain was the first K-pop star to break out internationally. In 2006, *Time* magazine named him one of the "100 Most Influential People Who Shape Our World." In 2007, he made *People* magazine's "most beautiful people" list.

MNET's Shin explained the formula for a K-pop hit. "If you look at the videos, there are two immediate attention grabs. The visual and the hook, you get them both at the same time." The biggest and most obvious difference, said Shin, is the quality of the dancing. "In the United States, with the popular bands, the choreography is very different." And by different he means bad.

"If you look at New Kids on the Block, for example, the members are not really synchronized. And in Justin Timberlake's [performances], the dancers are a bit off. Dancers in American bands are freer and go by feeling. The United States doesn't have singers who dance really well, unless it's someone like Michael Jackson, and that kind of talent comes around once in a hundred years. And J-pop bands don't dance well either; they don't practice."

Dancing well isn't enough. K-pop band members must dance in perfect synch, like clockwork. If you've ever seen a K-pop video, you'll notice that while no one is Baryshnikov, they do have split-second precision. And in order to achieve that, you have to put the band together while they're still young and hold off their debut until they've learned to act as one.

Shin added, "The K-pop practice duration is much longer than in the U.S. or with J-pop. The mentality in Korea is different. In Korea, if you're making a movie, you tell your staff, we have to sit up all night, and they do it. In Hollywood, however, they're strict about schedules. Same with music. The popularity of Korean music is tied to the fact that there's a strong collaborative mentality. They'll do it if it kills them."

The songs and videos focus on the singers and not on the musicians; there are no instrumental solos. As for the look of the K-pop video, it's worth noting that Psy's "Gangnam Style" is very atypical in that it uses real street scenes and real locations, mostly unadorned. The setting of most K-pop videos, by contrast, is sparse, futuristic, and sometimes wintry, like a space-age version of a Chekhov play. The girls always smile; the boys never do, instead bearing warrior expressions. Everyone is brutally attractive.

K-pop bands tend to have a relatively large number of members; Girls' Generation, for example, has nine. One doesn't need that many people to produce the simple K-pop sound, but South Korean music producers have found that large groups acting in unison are catnip to fans.

To get an idea of how manufactured K-pop is, one Korean television program started four simultaneous and separate K-pop bands with a color theme. Collectively, they are called the Color of K-pop. Two are girl bands: Dazzling Red and Mystic White. The other two are boy bands: Dramatic Blue and Dynamic Black. Band members wear outfits corresponding to the color in their band name. Each band has its own character: Mystic White is innocent, Dazzling Red is sassy, etc. Picture the Care Bears.

If this sounds like a marketing plan for mix-and-match shirts and pants of different colors at the Gap, that's exactly the effect the producers are going for. You don't need to know what the individual singers' back stories might be—which ones grew up in a trailer park or started singing gospel in their church. I mean, how interesting can a twenty-year-old's biography be, anyway? K-pop labels love stars, but not superstars: they don't want to get into a situation in which one band member becomes indispensable.

The bands are prefabricated and treated like a consumer product right from the beginning. Music producers create a product design for the band they want, right down to the precise look, sound, and marketing campaign, before they even audition members.

K-pop executives always have an eye on foreign markets, and adaptability to different cultures is part of the formula. Many K-pop bands release songs in Chinese or Japanese, like Girls' Generation's "Paparazzi" (nothing to do with Lady Gaga), recorded in Japanese. TVXQ!'s entire marketing strategy is based on appealing to Japan. Boy band Super Junior has a Chinese subunit, called Super Junior M, featuring two Chinese members. Many bands, like the girl group 2NE1, have Korean Americans so that the English sounds authentic. Clearly, the system works.

I asked Shin what he thought of Psy. He made a thoughtful observation: "The actor Bruce Lee changed westerners' ideas about Asians. And Psy is doing the same thing for Koreans."

He was careful to point out, though, as those in the K-pop industry are wont to do, that Psy is an outlier. It's not an insult—not anymore, at any rate. It's just that Korean music executives want the world to know there is more to Korean pop than Psy. "There are a lot more artists than you think," he said. "Psy is an example of a funny act; he's like Jack Black. But in the future, other people who are new and talented [will be successful globally]. At one time, UK pop culture invaded the world. So there is a lot of possibility for cultural migration."

Shin was entirely confident that K-pop could continue to break the language and culture barrier and become a huge global influence. "Music is very direct," he said. "Even if you don't know the lyrics, the sound goes into your inner ear and vibrates. The sound of a bass line moves your body; everyone reacts the same to this. Nationality and language can be overcome, because it's so directly felt. You can make instant friends with someone if you like the same music, even if you don't speak the same language. K-pop is beyond your imagination."

After much harassment and string-pulling, I was able to interview a bona fide K-pop idol (albeit via e-mail), Lee Joon, a member of the highly successful boy band MBLAQ. He's considered the cute one of the group, kind of like Harry Styles from the UK boy band One Direction. His immense popularity with girls is buoyed by his dance background; he was a dance major at the prestigious Korean National University of Arts.

Lee is a notable exception to the cookie-cutter K-pop star. In 2010, he publicly admitted that he suffers from bipolar disorder. In a country that is still loath to admit the existence of mental illness, his confession was groundbreaking. I told him that to many outsiders, all K-pop bands sound the same and asked him why he felt MBLAQ was unique.

"I think that in a way, it's to be expected that foreigners would think K-pop bands sound the same," he replied. "As for me, even I wouldn't claim that I'm completely dissimilar from other K-pop artists. But Korean artists are not all exactly alike. Each artist has his own distinct color and interests. So the genre really does contain a lot of variety."

The big unanswered question in K-pop is whether it can conquer the United States. Pop critic Lee Moon-won thinks so. "Something has changed in the United States. The Reagan era was the last time that the U.S. was exclusively into themselves. Before that, in the 1960s, foreign art house movies did really well in the United States. After that, in the 1970s and 1980s, at the height of the cold war, [the self-centeredness] was bad. Especially under Reagan. After Reagan, they became more open to other cultures."

Other observers don't see why breaking into the U.S. market is even a goal. Among them are Martina and Simon Stawski, an ebullient young Canadian couple and self-professed K-pop fanatics. Theirs is probably the best English-language site for comprehensive analyses and reviews of Korean culture.

In an interview in the couple's kooky bohemian studio in

Seoul, Martina said, "Look how well K-pop is doing in Japan. They buy the CDs for $40 a pop." The albums come with posters and other goodies. "But K-pop companies don't care about Asia. They want to break into America. I don't see why."

Simon and Martina agree that Korean record labels have to change their game plan if they want to appeal to the United States. Psy, they believe, is popular because he's funny.

"We think sometimes bands will try to go for humor in their videos, but it's *ehgyo* [cutesy baby talk] humor. *Ehgyo* humor is not easily understood [outside Asia]." She's right. It's not. It's sort of a setup in which a girl infantilizes herself as a means of light flirtation, and you can't tell whether she is talking to her older brother or her boyfriend. It's not quite French-style sexy-baby, like France Gall or Brigitte Bardot; it's more innocent, like a petulant child.

I asked Martina what suggestions she would make to Korean record companies, in order to broaden K-pop bands' appeal in the United States. She said, "They'd have to not use a lot of makeup for guys, the clothes can't be too tight, and then maybe some comedy. For some of the bands there are too many members." She suggested that having dual releases—one U.S. version and one local version—might be a solution.

If I had to pick a male band that had a good chance of crossover success, it would be Big Bang, and especially one member, G-Dragon, whose real name is Kwon Ji-young. (Dakota Fanning is reportedly a big fan.) G-Dragon was signed onto the SM label at age eight; he was a trainee there for five years. He then moved to the YG label, where he trained for an additional six years before debuting with Big Bang—meaning that he was in training for a total of about eleven years before setting foot on a public stage.

I saw G-Dragon perform live at the same concert where I saw Psy. When I first saw him on stage, I didn't know who he was or what to make of him. He arrived solo, which for some reason made me worried for him. He has a slight build with soft features, his eyes rimmed with black eyeliner. Tons of it. More than I used to wear even during the years when I listened to the Smiths and read Nietzsche.

He bellowed to the audience what the non-English-speaking world believes to be a universal rapper cry: "Whas-sup!" Then he led the audience in a neo-Dadaist chorus.

**G-DRAGON (IN ENGLISH):** When I say GET YOUR, you say CRAYON! GET YOUR!

**AUDIENCE:** Crayon!

**G-DRAGON:** GET YOUR!

**AUDIENCE:** Crayon!

What made this weird, in addition to already being weird, is that Korea didn't have crayons when I was growing up. It was a source of some wistfulness in my house, actually. The closest they had was Cray-pas, which is a more sophisticated pastel cousin of the crayon.

I wasn't sure I was hearing him correctly until I saw that the giant screen behind him showed images of crayons. And then he launched into one of his biggest hits, called "Crayon." Trust me, it's a good song.

## THE GANGNAM CHAINSAW MASSACRE

The adulation of K-pop stars had a bit of a dark side: it inevitably gave rise to legions of fans who were willing to go to extremes to look like their idols.

South Korea is the world's plastic surgery capital, in terms of procedures per capita, leaving countries like Brazil and the United States in the dust. In 2011, some 1.3 percent of Koreans had some kind of cosmetic procedure; this is 35 percent higher than the United States and nearly double that of Japan or France.[3] A figure like 1.3 percent might seem trivial, but not when you're in Seoul, where the vast majority of procedures are concentrated. Some one-fifth to one-third of women in Korea's capital (accounts vary) have undergone some kind of beauty-enhancing procedure. Apgujeong—my old neighborhood, located in the famous Gangnam district—is the absolute center of the plastic surgery hub. Though the neighborhood is smaller than one square mile in size, it contains some four hundred plastic surgery clinics.[4]

There is sort of a golden mean for Korean beauty, and it's wholly different from western standards. In North America and Europe, nose reduction and silicone lips are very popular. In Brazil, fat injections, including buttock augmentation, constitute 13.7 percent of all plastic surgery procedures.[5] In Korea, however, the request for any of those procedures is basically zero.

Next to articles about Samsung and Psy, the Korean obsession with cosmetic surgery is probably the most oft-reported Korean story in the western press, and the stories are framed with condescension and horror. Frequently they take the angle that Koreans are trying to look white, and these procedures are some kind of racial reassignment surgery. What utter rot.

I have had one plastic surgery procedure, the double-eyelid surgery, by which a crease is created in each eyelid to make the eyes appear rounder and larger. It's the most frequently requested cosmetic operation in Korea, unlike North America and Europe, where breast augmentation is the top procedure.

Dr. Kim Byung-gun, director of BK Plastic Surgery Hospital in Seoul, said the double-eyelid procedure accounts for some 30 to 40 percent of his practice. Double-eyelid surgery is almost mandatory for Korean celebrities. In fact, the Korean R & B singer Rain has said in interviews that his handlers warned him that his refusal to get double-eyelid surgery would kill his career. He held out.

I caved. But I promise I look no more Caucasian now than I did the day I was born, and I have hard evidence of this: no westerner noticed.

The procedure in a Seoul clinic took twenty-five minutes, required no incisions, and left no scarring. It cost about $1,000. Just three stitches on each eyelid, which resulted in the creation of a discreet crease. A week later, when I returned to my home—Germany, at the time—none of my non-Asian friends caught on until I pointed it out.

So why bother doing it? I'm just vain. It's kind of like that old saw that women dress up not for men but to impress other women. Asians, for the most part, get the double-eyelid surgery for themselves and for each other—not for white people.

When a westerner thinks of the ideal for female beauty, the term "egg-shaped face" probably doesn't come to mind. I don't recall Shakespeare's sonnets or the Songs of Solomon comparing their ladylove to any poultry product. But according to prominent Seoul-based plastic surgeon Dr. Rhee Se-whan, Koreans have considered the egg-shaped face (wider proportions on top, tapering to a narrow chin) a thing of beauty since time immemorial. Some Koreans will undergo "facial bone contouring" to achieve this ideal, which can include sawing down the jawbone to make the face look less square-shaped. The procedure is almost never performed in the west.

Yet the procedure is not as invasive as you might think. According to Dr. Kim Byung-gun, the jaw contouring, called mandible angle reduction surgery, does use a rotating buzz saw one centimeter in diameter, but its point of entry is within the mouth, not on the face, so the procedure leaves no outwardly visible scarring. It takes an hour, and runs between $5,000 and $6,000. "It's very safe, not a risky surgery," said Dr. Kim. "Nobody notices." That seems to be the catchword for most of the procedures Koreans favor: nobody notices. Discretion is the name of the game.

Peculiarly, even though breast augmentation has become increasingly popular in Korea, the enlargement is intentionally subtle, says Dr. Kim. Basically, if people notice a difference right away, you've gone too far.

After double-eyelid surgery, the most commonly requested procedure in most Korean clinics is rhinoplasty. Nose jobs are popular in the west, too, but to achieve different ends. Westerners almost invariably want smaller noses (and in the last few years, narrower at the nostril area). The perfect nose by Korean standards, however, has particular contours. Dr. Rhee drew a geometric diagram, explaining that, for a woman, the bottom of the nose should not be so flat that it is at a 90-degree angle to the mouth. "That looks too masculine. Ideally you want something between a 95- and a 100-degree angle." Furthermore, the profile of the nose itself should be more acute in a woman's nose, so rhinoplasty might include adding a cartilage tip to make the nose pointier.

The nose bridge—the part of the nose that falls between or just below the eyes—is what keeps spectacles from sliding off your face, and it's a particular preoccupation for Koreans, who tend to have very small bridges. Though one Korean dermatologist cited Princess Diana as an example of someone with a prominent bridge, all the medical professionals I talked to insisted that Koreans were not hankering for a western nose. "We cannot make an Asian nose into a European or Caucasian nose," said Dr. Kim emphatically. "We're not trying to. For Asians to have a Caucasian nose is not pretty."

Another cultural factor that explains why Korean plastic surgeons really had to perfect their craft, according to

Dr. Rhee Se-whan, is that "Koreans really pay a lot of attention to people around them. In the west, people don't care if you marry twice or even three times. Well, at least, they don't care as much [as Koreans do]. In Korea, however, people always ask you, 'How old are you,' 'What does your boyfriend do for a living,' 'Where is your house.' Anyone in their line of vision is fair game for questions about their private lives. It's hard to say whether this is good or bad. But in the context of plastic surgery, let's say someone gets double-eyelid surgery. People won't say, 'It looks great!' They'll say, 'Hmm . . . it looks kind of asymmetrical.' Korean women especially."

Has Korea gone too far with its plastic surgery fanaticism? I would say that it's an unimportant question except for one troubling trend Dr. Rhee mentioned: the increase in the number of young children requesting surgery.

"When I was a kid," said Dr. Rhee, "no one got plastic surgery. Even in college, there weren't that many. But even now, middle-school children get plastic surgery during their winter school break. It's not considered weird. It's considered normal."

The phenomenon of underage surgery is particularly dangerous because children are highly susceptible to peer pressure and the desire to conform. In some affluent schools, this has led to a surgical arms race—a one-upmanship among schoolchildren to look prettier, like a diabolical version of buying the trendiest autumn clothes for the new school year.

Rhee gave an example. "There was a plain middle-school girl who got surgery and got much better looking. She got to go out with the best-looking guy in the school, so her friend [wanted surgery], too."

You might be wondering where all these standards for perfect proportion come from. Who calibrates these magic rulers, protractors, and color samples that determine the golden mean of what constitutes the right face? Well, if you were to assemble all the various descriptions of what Koreans find beautiful—narrow face, alabaster skin, etc.—you would find that the Platonic ideal of Korean beauty is based on the features most closely associated with North Korean women.

# 9

# NORTHERN GIRLS, SOUTHERN BOYS

• • • • • • • • • • • • • •

IN APRIL 2013 TENSIONS BETWEEN NORTH AND South Korea were at their most severe since the end of the Korean War. As head of the Korean Tourist Organization, Lee Charm was not thrilled with the effect of this threat on Korean tourism. Many South Koreans are familiar and weary of this recurring game. The north makes veiled threats of annihilation almost every time there is a new South Korean regime, and since President Park Geun-hye had just taken office two months prior, the north's saber-rattling was on schedule.

Lee, like most South Korean officials, approaches the issue coolly. "The North Korean regime is not crazy. They are very calculating. They don't observe any rules; they use extortion. Basically, they're a criminal organization, but not crazy."

Lee believes, as do the vast majority of South Koreans, that North Koreans are not so stupid that they fail to see the likelihood of mutually assured destruction if war breaks out.

"They know if they start conflict, they will be eliminated right away. That would mean the end of their regime. But they also know the world is very weak in the face of someone who doesn't play by the rules. They know they can get a good deal no matter what."

By "good deal," Lee is referring to the world's worst-kept secret: North Korea makes these threats to extort money from the rest of the world, in the form of "humanitarian aid."

South Korea's fear of North Korea has diminished over the years, as evidenced by a popular television chat show called *Now on My Way to Meet You*, which features a panel of gorgeous North Korean female refugees. It would be only a slight exaggeration to say that *Now on My Way to Meet You* is the most emotionally confusing program in the worldwide history of television.

Watching this show makes you feel as though you are flipping television channels between *The Lawrence Welk Show*, the Miss Universe pageant, and *Schindler's List*. The format is part chat show: sometimes the North Korean beauties discuss cute and humorous topics, like the trials of dating South Korean men. It's also part variety show, with the women displaying their talents at dancing, singing, or playing the accordion (a bizarrely popular instrument in North Korea). The third and crucial component of the show are the women's harrowing testimonies of torture, rape, starvation, and other hardships they endured, not only in North Korea but during their escape as well.

I asked the show's producer, Lee Jin-min, why her show's panel guests were all women. She made reference to an ancient Korean expression, "Northern girls, southern boys." It refers to the common local stereotype that the prettiest Korean women are to be found in the north, whereas the handsomest Korean men are to be found in the south.

The show's creators felt that the audience would respond more sympathetically to women than to men. "South Koreans feel very benevolently toward North Korean women. Nonetheless, in practice, many South Koreans are still not totally ready to accept northern refugees [settling permanently in the South]. In order to put forth the most positive image of the refugees, we determined that women would be more suitable for the show."

But the show does an important public service: it helps to combat the discrimination that North Korean refugees suffer in South Korea. Many locals harbor resentment that their tax money is being spent accommodating the refugees. South Koreans worry whether their economy can withstand the rapidly growing influx of refugees and the separate welfare category it creates. Some northern refugees are disabled or in poor health; some possess no job skills that would be useful outside a totalitarian regime.

The North Korean guests on *Now on My Way to Meet You* look anything but sick and desperate.

No other country on earth could have produced a show like this. In typical Korean talk show fashion, the women have worked with a stylist and are dressed to the nines in coordinated, knee-length silk dresses whose pastel colors are carefully chosen so as not to clash with each other and to create a tableau that is pleasing as a whole. Their hair is glossy and coiffed in the latest styles, and they are sitting demurely with their legs closed and poised in an identical formation. If you didn't understand Korean and you didn't know what you were watching, you'd think they were discussing the new line of Gucci handbags. But it soon becomes apparent that the glamorous image is completely incongruous with the tales that come out of the girls' mouths.

Take the story of Yoon Ah-young. She told her story on a May 2013 episode of *Now on My Way to Meet You*.

In 1998 she and her family escaped to China, smuggled in by one of the many human traffickers who specialize in this area. The trafficker told Yoon that she had to be separated from her parents to better ensure her safety. Instead, the human smuggler sold the seventeen-year-old girl into slavery for 4,000 Chinese yuan ($650), to a family who wanted a nanny.

Yoon was beaten by the female head of the house, who would tell her, "You're an illegal. No one cares if you live or die. You don't matter." She stayed in captivity with this family for three years. "For those three years, I had only one goal that kept me alive. I just wanted to save enough money to buy a gun, a quiet one, and then I'd kill her and then kill myself." One day, Yoon packed a bag, intending never to return. She was worried that the sound of her shoes would wake the old woman, so she made her escape barefoot.

She reunited with her parents, and in 2004 they reached the promised land, South Korea. Defectors who speak out publicly risk putting their loved ones in jeopardy back home. For this reason, many defectors choose to keep a low profile.

Several refugees I approached initially agreed to let me interview them, but got nervous and backed out.

I did manage to interview one of the show's panelists, Shin Eun-hee, who had also escaped from North Korea to China with her family in 1998, when she was twelve years old. I asked Shin why she was brave enough to appear on *Now on My Way to Meet You*—and to talk to an American journalist like me. Shin explained: "All twenty-four thousand of us North Korean refugees are in danger. And it's especially unsafe to talk about North Korea to the press. But there's an expression: 'You can't avoid making fermented bean paste just because you're worried about maggots.' I'm not going to give up my work just because I'm afraid of North Korea."

Her parents were Christians practicing in secret—presumably having come under the influence of a handful of South Korean ministers who sneak into the north to spread the gospel. Preaching Christianity in North Korea can lead to a death sentence, and their proselytes are often executed or put into labor camps. "The reason we had to leave North Korea is that my parents were distributing cassette tapes about Christianity, and somehow they were discovered. We got caught by a government agent, but we managed to elude him and fled to China." Shin is one of the very lucky refugees whose family managed to stay together in the escape.

Originally, Shin's family had no intention of making their way to South Korea; they expected to live out their days in China. This is fairly common among North Korean émigrés, despite the fact that they live in fear of being arrested by

Chinese authorities and returned to North Korea—per agreement between the two countries, which are still allies despite increasing mutual annoyance.

Why stay in China, then? Because South Korea is not considered a livable option by many North Koreans. "In North Korea," said Shin, "we were always taught that South Korea was very poor. But when we were living in China, we realized that Chinese worshiped South Korea like gods. That's when we started hoping to move to South Korea."

Shin's story is a fine example of the unexpected far-reaching effects of Hallyu. The Chinese veneration of South Korea partly stems from the popularity of "Korean cool," and that obviously comes from Korea's success in technology, business, and pop culture. Without this Hallyu-induced fantasy about South Korea, Shin's family and others like them might have remained living illegally in China, forever fearing that they would be caught and sent back to North Korea.

Now that Shin has been immersed in Hallyu—right down to being a television personality in her own right—she says, "I'm proud to be Korean."

I asked Shin a question I was almost sure she would not answer: what did she miss about North Korea? In the Korea of my youth, when dictator Chun Doo-hwan was president, it was illegal to express anything that could be interpreted as sympathy toward North Korea. Had this interview occurred in, say, 1985, I could have been jailed for asking the question and Shin could have been jailed for answering it—political asylum status notwithstanding.

Her answer was touching and typically Korean in its

open sentimentality: "I miss my hometown, our home, friends, school, neighbors, teacher, the air, and the tree we planted in front of our house. We just left everything as it was. I never got to say good-bye. I miss my hometown so much that I can hardly breathe. This one time when I was walking to school, I slipped on a rock in the road. I even miss that rock. I still think about the schoolyard where I played with my friends. I could walk from home to there in ten minutes; now I wouldn't even get there if I walked ten years. There is no end to how much I miss it."

Shin, who is working toward a career in broadcasting, seems to be flourishing and well-integrated into South Korean society; she doesn't even have a North Korean accent anymore. She is aware of her good fortune. "People who were born into freedom don't think there's anything special about it," she said. "But the freedom one gets from painful effort is very special indeed. What I love best about South Korea is that it gave me this special type of freedom."

Most rational people don't believe they can be brainwashed. Yet I think I have been. Whenever I talk or write about North Korea, I have an involuntary physiological reaction. I can actually taste something bitter in my mouth, even as I write these lines. It's the result of years of anticommunist terror instilled in me during my years in South Korea. When I see pictures of any of the North Korean Kim dynasty, I am terrified.

South Korea's official stance on North Korea has changed

dramatically since the 1980s. When I lived in Korea, we were basically led to believe that North Korea was the spawn of an orgy between Satan, Beelzebub, Emperor Nero, and Pol Pot. This sentiment has since evolved into "Stop discriminating against North Korean refugees who choose to settle in our country. Especially the women; they're hot."

I'm having a hard time adapting to the new open-mindedness. My 1980s-era South Korean education guaranteed that North Korea would always be the stuff of nightmares for me, a terror buried deep in the unreachable, inalterable region of my brain.

Nowadays, North Korea is the focus of both fascination and hatred, and the butt of jokes by the likes of the American animated TV show *South Park*. Its late leader, Kim Jong-il, remains, so far, the most media-exposed of the three generations of Kims who have ruled the country. Kim Jong-il's life and legacy is the stuff of surreal legend both at home and abroad.

In his native North Korea, he is celebrated as a man of many superlatives, including being the alleged world record holder for the most holes in one in a single golf game—eleven out of eighteen holes, and that was on his very first time ever on the green, according to his official biography. He has never made a bowel movement, supposedly. Kim Jong-il also invented the hamburger. Almost touchingly, North Koreans have a lot of pride in their heritage, though it's for absurd reasons. The few foreigners who have been permitted to tour North Korea report bizarre trivia passed on to them by some pretty unironic local tour guides: Koreans are such a glorious race that they created not only the world's great technological innovations but also the spoon.

Though this all sounds hilarious, I'm certain that North Koreans would never dream of laughing at any of it. Outside Korea, meanwhile, it's easy to make a laughingstock of a man who was the world's largest importer of Hennessy whiskey and sported the worst male perm in the history of human hair.

Equally dumbfounding is the combination of gall and clownish insanity demonstrated by members of his family. Kim Jong-il's eldest son, Kim Jong-nam, tried to enter Japan on a Dominican Republic passport in 2001, for the purpose of visiting Disneyland Tokyo.[1] So maybe it's starting to make sense that he got passed over for the leadership role, which instead went to his younger brother, the hapless Kim Jong-un.

When it comes to the way that South Koreans view North Korea, it's an altogether different story. I cannot really appreciate the irony and surrealism of North Korean buffoonery. My deepest fears cannot simply adapt to the times. When I lived in Korea, the atmosphere was thick with what I now realize was paranoia. Some tall buildings had signs near the hall windows saying that, for reasons of national security, it was illegal to take photographs from the windows. The fear was that such photos could fall into the hands of North Korean spies, just in case those spies were particularly interested in a view of the parking lot.

Most schools that I knew held an annual Anti-Communist Speech Contest. At my school, it was the only kind of speech contest there was. You cannot know how it feels to see a first-grade boy with a bowl haircut stand on a pulpit in front of thousands of students, shaking his fist like Mussolini and shouting at the top of his lungs, "We shall obliterate the North Korean Communist regime!" At which point the audience would roar and clap.

I'm pretty sure first prize was just an embossed certificate, but from the way these kids were getting into those speeches, you'd think their lives and their families' lives depended on it. I never, ever heard a fellow student laugh about these speeches, not even once. Not even when I was hanging out with my friends on our own time, off school grounds. Once I said something like, "Can't they have a speech contest on some other topic?" Everyone looked at me quizzically. I thought they would be impressed or at least scared by my revolutionary bravado. Instead, they just thought I was some weird American girl. That was the last time I expressed my true opinion on anything while a student at a Korean school.

Every semester in art class, we had to make anti-Communist posters. I cannot think of anything at which I was less talented. Making anti-Communist posters is like learning to speak a foreign language without an accent: age twelve is already way too old to start learning. I had no idea how to write a slogan or what kind of illustration was supposed to go with it. But no matter how cynical and smart I thought I was, no matter how much I scoffed, the lesson of fear seeped into me anyway.

There's an ancient rule of human nature, reiterated in

some form by everyone from the Greeks to Shakespeare to Carl Jung: you become what you hate and fear most. This is what happened to South Korea during the cold war. The country was so afraid of the north's propaganda that South Korea developed a propaganda campaign of its own. It was not nearly as extreme as the north's, but some of the rhetoric had a similar ring.

Imagine someone telling you over and over again that something is evil, but without ever really giving you any concrete information about it. The combination of repetition and absence of information make you increasingly scared. That's what my education on North Korea was like.

I never, not ever, not once, saw photos of Kim Il-sung, even though the rest of the world had access to them. South Korean media only ran sketches of him; it was feared that real photos would humanize him and possibly be appropriated for propaganda by communist sympathizers in the north. As a result of the absence of any images, he is the phantom that haunts my dreams. This photo embargo has now been lifted; after the elder Kim died in 1994, the media gradually began to show photographs of his son and successor, Kim Jong-il.

There was much more media coverage of Kim Jong-il than of his father, not just in South Korea but in the world at large. Which is probably why I was far less afraid of the younger Kim. He lacked his father's charisma, looks, and gravitas. The scion's maladroitness and inability to look good in a beige jumpsuit made him a lot less threatening. I'm not alone in thinking that he was the most interesting member of the family. You have to respect a despot who isn't such a workaholic that he forgets to develop some hobbies.

Kim Jong-il had real cultural ambitions. He was a known cinephile who fancied himself a rare blend of canny Hollywood producer and serious film auteur—even authoring a film theory book called *The Art of Cinema* in 1973, followed by *The Cinema and the Art of Directing* in 1987. He offers such insights as "Language is extremely important in literature" and "Compose the plot correctly."

Dissatisfied with North Korea's propaganda films, which he apparently admitted were artistically substandard, this François Truffaut of northern Asia did what any self-respecting film producer would do in that situation: in 1978, he arranged for the abduction of South Korea's top film director, Shin Sang-ok, and his actress ex-wife, Choi Eun-hee. He had them brought to Pyongyang and forced them to make Cannes-caliber propaganda films for him. In Kim's own mind, this howling human rights abuse was just the logical extension of his enthusiasm for his hobbies.

When I was at school, North Korean studies were taught in a class called *doduk*, which means "correct conduct." (Some prefer to translate it as "moral education.") Ordinary Korean students considered it an easy *A*; for me, it was one of my worst subjects.

The class, offered from first grade through the end of high school, was an education of the soul and spirit—basically, tips on how not to be a sociopath. It included lessons and parables on how to conduct oneself as a good citizen, the importance of being respectful of elders, being gentle with nature (mostly trees—they didn't care about animals at all), and basic etiquette. However, there was a thinly veiled agenda. Hong Weonil, head of public affairs at the National Institute for International Education (one of the people I embarrassed with my Starbucks cup), said that *doduk* was originally created as a way for Korea's previous iron-fisted leaders to peddle their agenda. Previously, it was called *kookmin yulli*—citizenship ethics. "It was created to justify the political dictatorship and political propaganda. After the country became more democratic, they changed the curriculum," said Hong.

My most vivid memory of *doduk* was the creepy watercolor illustrations in the textbook. They were an adult's idea of what a child's painting would look like, and as a result they looked as though they were painted by someone inside an insane asylum. A typical image was a tableau of South Korean farmers gaily tilling the soil. There were also quite a few vivid drawings of Seoul getting bombed to bits during the Korean War.

Many of the lessons taught in *doduk* are hard to disagree with, such as a gripping parable about a persimmon tree, wherein the moral was that if you cut off all the branches, it will stop bearing fruit. Only later did I realize that all this "don't be a stupid jerk" section of the class was just padding. It was a delivery vehicle for the real raison d'être of the *doduk* class: to make a hard sell that communism was an imminent and evil threat.

The books contained frightening fictional stories illustrative of how bleak life was in the north. In one such story, which I believe was in the sixth-grade textbook, a boy in North

Korea idiotically asks his grandfather what life was like before communism. The grandfather waxes nostalgic about old
Korea. A few days later, the grandfather gets dragged off by
the communists for his failure to keep his opinions to himself.
For a twelve-year-old with no access to any other information
on North Korea, this was terrifying stuff.

What we were taught was historically accurate. We learned
that the founder of the North Korean state, Kim Il-sung,
rose to power shortly after Korea was liberated from Japan at
the end of World War II. He declared himself the true leader
of the Korean peninsula and formed a cult of personality
around himself, modeled after that of his mentor, Joseph
Stalin. He sent all political undesirables, especially Koreans
who had collaborated with the Japanese, to labor camps or
he had them executed. He was like a Bond villain.

I was relieved and a little surprised that starting in 2010,
the Korean Ministry of Education made the radical move of
issuing brand-new textbooks that expunged most of the content pertaining to what they called "peace studies." In other
words, the texts finally moved past their cold war propaganda. The official ministry announcement at the time stated
that the new texts have cut "content that discusses South Korea's economic superiority. . . . They will be based on objective facts. Rather than exaggerating the negative aspects of
the North Korean system, the texts will also discuss the north's
positive aspects. . . . We will move past our Cold War perspective on North Korea, and most likely 'unification studies'
will give way to 'security studies.' "[2] This is a far cry from the
nightmare-inducing watercolors of yore.

The ministry also replaced outdated terms with more politically correct ones. Significantly, North Koreans who have escaped to South Korea are no longer to be called "defectors"; instead, they are "North Korean émigrés." All of these changes reflect the rapidly evolving attitudes of South Koreans toward North Koreans. The new motto seems to be, hate the regime but not its people.

I have to say, though, that just like corporal punishment and stool samples, growing up with the fear of invasion is something that forever sets you apart from other people. For me, at least, the fact that the North Korean threat was very real made it fun to me, a sheltered American kid who had previously never got to do anything more exciting at school than a tornado drill.

Periodically, North Korean aircraft would airdrop little packs of chewing gum or candy over Seoul; these were wrapped in notes containing North Korean propaganda. The school told us that if we were ever to find such an object, we were to turn it in to the principal immediately and absolutely not read or open it. I am devastated to report that I never found one.

# 10

# K-DRAMA: TELEVISION AND THE ORIGINS OF HALLYU

· · · · · · · · · · · · · · · ·

WHEN I LIVED IN KOREA, THE ONLY ENGLISH-language television channel at the time was the American Forces Korea Network.[1] I watched a lot of ancient American reruns on AFKN, including the 1960s sitcom *Gidget*, in which Sally Field played a fifteen-and-a-half-year-old California teen.

I was dumbfounded by the banality of the scrapes Gidget would get herself into week after week, like losing her surfboard and having to get a new one, or having to go on two different dates on the same night. It was an utterly alien world to me. When did she study for exams? Why did her father let her wear a bikini? And why was 1960s Californian civilization light-years ahead of 1980s Korea?

Shows like *Gidget* highlighted one of the main differences between American society and Korean society during the time that I lived there: teenage dating culture. Today, dating among pre-university kids is much more common in Korea, but when I was in school, I didn't know anyone who was given official permission by their parents to have a boyfriend or girlfriend. If you wanted to date you had to do it on the sly, and for most of us it was really just too much trouble. Consequently, Koreans would begin college with no notion of how to do something as basic as asking someone out to dinner, let alone arranging an assignation of any kind. In my neighborhood, Apgujeong, a boy who liked a girl would signal this by giving her an orange—at the time, an expensive fruit in Korea. Hence the nickname the media assigned to Gangnam kids from my generation: the "Orange Clan."

Kids who came of age in the 1980s and 1990s were part of a hilariously awkward generation that was transitioning between marriages arranged by matchmakers and the western notion of dating that is commonplace in Korea today. They had no idea how to meet people of the opposite sex, so they sought mates the only way they knew how—via ridiculously contrived and elaborate meetups called *sogae-ting. Sogae* is the Korean word for "introduction"; *ting* is not Korean at all—it is actually pseudo-English. Koreans seemed to think that *ting* was a proper abbreviation for the English word "dating." I'm not kidding. Ergo, every dating-related activity had the suffix *-ting* at the end of it.

There were many variations on *sogae-ting*, some of which resembled live-action role-playing games. One popular one was called *elevator-ting*, which required monopolizing the elevator of a random high-rise commercial building. Groups of girls would stand on different floors of the building, in front of the elevator banks. Boys would be inside the elevator, riding up and down and stopping at each floor. If, when the el-

evator doors opened, you liked the look of a girl, you'd get off
on that floor and start talking to her. It was so ridiculous that
it could never be construed as threatening or predatory, and
that was the whole point. For the people who worked in the
building, it was pretty annoying to have an entire elevator go
out of commission for half a day.

Another popular form of *sogae-ting* was called *007-ting*, as in
James Bond 007, so-called because it required a little sleuthing
and stealth. For example, a girl might be given the following
instructions: "Go to the KFC in Gangnam and find the boy
who is talking to the statue of Colonel Sanders." If you didn't
fancy the boy talking to the Colonel, you could discreetly disappear without embarrassing him face-to-face.

These kinds of antics, I am told, have gone by the wayside: nowadays, if a boy fancies a girl, he asks her out on a
date like a normal human being. But in that repressed period of psychotically complicated dating rituals, it's not hard
to understand why I loved shows like *Gidget*, as well as more
contemporary shows featuring American teen life, such as
*Charles in Charge* and *The Cosby Show*. I began to worship the
United States, the country of my birth, which I had previously deemed uninhabitably hostile and racist.

AFKN didn't air regular commercials to hock dishwash-
ing liquid or Barbies; instead, they ran military-oriented ads
with service messages like "Don't resell items from the Commissary on the local black market," "Don't mail explosives,"
and a lot of ads about OPSEC—operation security, for which
the slogan was "Loose lips sink ships." Because most of my
television viewing was on this U.S. military network, I grew

up believing that Korea was very much dependent on this superpower for our every need—safety and good television.

Today, Seoul has a bright self-assuredness and self-love. An advertisement from any company worth its salt features Korean models and celebrities. When I lived in Seoul, however, cosmetic and clothing companies preferred Caucasian models with such pitiful desperation that they recruited western students I knew from the international school, many of them unattractive.

The Eighth U.S. Army base in the Yongsan district of Seoul was like a glistening city on a hill. It occupied prime Seoul real estate, and while the rest of Seoul was jam-packed with skyscrapers and traffic with barely an inch of free space, Yongsan had an eighteen-hole golf course, the only Burger King in Seoul with its own parking lot, and housing with real backyards. The commissary and PX were the only places in Seoul where you could get cheese, turkey, and underarm deodorant. All these items and more made their way to the black markets, where ordinary Koreans could buy them at three times the price. It was highly illegal, and these black markets were constantly shutting down, moving, and reopening.

The neighborhood surrounding the military base was a microeconomy that slavishly served GIs, and was a den of hawkers shouting in bad English to draw shoppers in to buy counterfeit Polo shirts—one fellow of local legend always yelled, "Everything is free!" At night, the streets were infested with hideous hookers with giant bad perms and ghoulish face powder.

In recent years the U.S. military base has reduced its presence in Korea, citing budget cuts and probably shifting priorities to the "war on terror; only twenty-five thousand troops are stationed there now, about half as many as during the cold war. The United States is turning over the Yongsan base in Seoul to the Korean government, which is transforming the space into a series of large public parks. As a result of this transformation, the surrounding areas no longer look like a sad scene from *Full Metal Jacket* or some other American film about wartime Vietnam, with shifty locals sycophantically catering to soldiers' pleasures.

But in the 1980s, Koreans worshiped, feared, and resented the United States. Korean university students staged violent protests—including an absurd number of self-immolations—against the U.S. military presence. The protests were focused on ousting President Chun Doo-hwan, who served from 1980 to 1988; but since he was thought by some to be a lackey of the United States, anti-Americanism was always stated or implied.

Of course, in between shouting "Down with the Yanks," many of those very students were applying to graduate schools in the evil imperialist United States. As ultimate proof that Koreans couldn't possibly hate the United States as much as they sometimes claimed, Korean television networks aired a fair number of American programs dubbed into Korean, and audiences gobbled them up.

My classmates loved shows with heroic, macho leads like the *A-Team* and *Airwolf.* For grown-ups, there were old Hollywood films and modern adaptations of Sidney Sheldon novels.

The United States looked so appealing in those shows, and Koreans watched them with envy and aspiration.

Cultural critic Lee Moon-won claims that Koreans' attachment to U.S. shows up until the 1980s had little genuine affection behind it; rather, he says, it was a form of political conditioning. "In the old days, we didn't watch American dramas because we loved the shows. During the cold war, America was the leader of the free world, so everyone worshiped America, and U.S. culture spread everywhere."

But the Korean preference for American dramas wasn't just about politics. Let's be honest: until the 1990s, Korean dramas were provincial and tedious. Production values were really poor and the plots focused on minute domestic issues. All dramas used to be produced in-house at the television networks by stables of writers and producers who were either not trying very hard or suffering from creative fatigue. Apparently, the government shared my sentiments.

In typical fashion, Korea's politicians and lawmakers took abrupt and drastic action to improve K-drama quality. The Investment Broadcasting Law, enacted in 1990, required Korean terrestrial (nonsatellite) networks to purchase a certain percentage of their programs from independent production companies (initially 2 percent; this grew to 20 percent over the years).[2]

Just as the American television scene was permanently transformed at the turn of the millennium by risk-taking private networks like HBO—resulting in shows like *The Sopranos*, which raised the standard for all American TV—so did the inclusion of obscure self-employed writers and producers, who breathed new life into K-dramas in the 1990s. Breaking from the formula of relatively buttoned-down American dramas, K-dramas unleashed their inner *han* in an abundance of screaming, crying, eye-clawing, on-screen physical violence and unfettered emotion.

## THE DIPLOMATIC POUCH

Hallyu was born, some say, in a diplomatic pouch that was shuttled between Seoul and Hong Kong in 1992. And the contents of the pouch? No, not a secret microfilm, but a Betamax tape of a Korean television drama called *What Is Love*. Obviously. What else would two Korean civil servants be sending to each other using surreptitious means?

The sender of the Betamax was Chung Injoon, a career civil servant and cultural attaché who now serves as visiting fellow at the Korea Culture and Tourism Institute (KCTI is a government organization); the recipient was the Korean consulate in Hong Kong.

Their mission: to get this show on Hong Kong television by any means necessary. In so doing, Chung told me, "I witnessed the first signs of the Korean Wave." Not only witnessed it, but set it in motion. At the time, he was the director of the overseas division of the KCTI, which in those days was called the Korean Overseas Information Service. Chung had to use a diplomatic pouch because of protocols that made it a logistical nightmare to ship broadcast-quality videos between borders. "We thought, maybe it will be opened, maybe it won't," he recalled. If the parcel had been intercepted, it would have been confiscated. And that might have changed the course of Hallyu history.

*What Is Love*, which tells the story of two middle-class, middle-aged housewives who've been friends since high school, enjoyed a 50 percent audience share for its time slot in Korea (personal note: I think it's boring). Chung and his partners in crime at the Korean consulate realized that by airing the show on a single network—Hong Kong's ATV—it could reach not just Hong Kong but also neighboring Guangdong Province in mainland China, for a combined potential audience of 50 million in a densely populated, highly compact area.

In those days, there was no demand for Korean television shows, not even in Asia. It was going to be an uphill battle to convince a Hong Kong station to pick up the show. In order to ensure the network would not have an excuse to say no, Chung and the consulate's office convinced Korean companies in Hong Kong to buy ad time during the shows and used Korean government funds to dub it into Cantonese, at no small expense.

Their efforts paid off: ATV started airing the show. It became so popular in the region that during the time slots that it aired on Thursday and Saturday evening, "there were no people or cars on the street," according to Chung; everyone was at home watching the show.

Furthermore, the series caused a cultural ripple in Hong Kong society, said Chung, introducing Korean Confucian concepts of spousal roles. "In those days in Hong Kong, the husband cooked dinner after work. But the show sabotaged this, displaying the father as a superpower. When they watched the show, they saw the wife cooking, which caused kind of a syndrome."

I'm not at all sure that this was the kind of cultural transmission Koreans had in mind, but regardless, the seeds of an addiction were planted. The show got picked up by mainland China's CCTV. A slew of other Korean dramas followed; their popularity spread throughout Asia—Japan, Vietnam, Malaysia, and the Philippines.

In the Philippines over the last fifteen years, Koreanovelas have replaced South American telenovelas in popularity, spawning the Philippines' own soap opera industry. Not only are the K-dramas inherently popular, they have also inspired about a dozen Filipino remakes with local casts and in Tagalog.

On a recent trip to Seoul, I met some Filipino chefs from the Center for Culinary Arts (CAA) in Manila. They were in Korea on a reconnaissance mission: they wanted to open a Korean restaurant in Manila. I asked them why Filipinos were so crazy about Korean dramas.

"It has a little of everything: comedy, drama, action," said Tim Abejuela, a chef instructor. He added that Filipinos relate to the plots of K-dramas: "[In the Philippines], we have the same caste system. Koreans go through the same things as Filipinos do. Korean parents are pushy; they want to choose who you marry. Filipinos love the drama—hard-core slapping, dragging the hair, and cat fights—they love that." Regarding the Filipino remakes of K-dramas, Abejuela said, "They do it with our own actors, and in Tagalog, but [Filipinos] still prefer the Korean [originals]."

K-dramas are now beloved by Asia as a whole. In Taiwan, the airtime devoted to Korean dramas was getting so out of control that in 2012, Taiwan's National Communications Commission called upon a Taiwanese network to reduce its primetime showings of Korean programs and increase the number of hours devoted to non-Korean shows.[3]

Korean dramas also have huge audiences in Latin America—perhaps because of their emotional similarity to telenovelas. In South America, Korean dramas have become hits in Brazil, Chile, and Argentina. In Paraguay, some Korean dramas were dubbed not only in Spanish but also in the indigenous local dialect of Guarani.

In 2013, Cubans became obsessed with the Korean drama series *Queen of Housewives*, which airs four times a week on the state-run Canal Habana.[4] The Cuban press reported that when one of the show's heartthrob male stars, Yoon Sang-hyun, visited Havana on a promotional tour in November, he was mobbed at the airport by a crowd of hyped-up Cuban female fans. A Cuban national network airing a Korean soap is especially odd since Cuba and Korea have no diplomatic ties; in fact, Cuba has never screened a Korean movie. Yet for some reason, the Korea Trade-Investment Promotion Agency (KOTRA), a government-run trade group, has an office in Havana.

Does this smell of government involvement? Yes, and they're not embarrassed about it. According to the Korean network MBC, the drama was dubbed in Spanish with the assistance of KOTRA. That is, with public funds. One can't help wondering whether Korea is waiting for communism to topple so it can swoop in with Korean cars and mobile phones.

K-dramas are soft power in action; they subtly and overtly promote Korean values, images, and tastes to their international audience. Owing to their popularity, the Korean look espoused by K-dramas—including pale, powdery skin and foundation for men—has become faddish in Korea. The Korean cosmetics industry has enjoyed a boom in Asia; one beauty chain alone, Face Shop, has a thousand stores throughout Asia. Obviously, the cosmetics companies employ the most popular Korean actors and singers to promote their products.

## THE DEATH OF MUST-SEE TV

The popularity of Korean dramas cannot all be ascribed to government conspiracy, however. One indication that global audiences are flocking to K-dramas of their own initiative is the tremendous success of DramaFever, a video-on-demand Internet portal that airs primarily Korean dramas, all subtitled in English. Founded in 2009 with a little seed money, the tiny New York–based operation has already started to generate annual revenues "in the seven figures," according to Seung Bak, the Korean American cofounder of the company. The site gets 6 million to 8 million unique visitors per month, but only 15 percent of those Korean American demographic viewers are from Asia. Nor are they Korean American. As

Bak says, "The demographic is too small." In fact, the majority of DramaFever's viewers are spread throughout the globe. Bak believes that in theory the site could flourish without any Korean subscribers at all.

Bak is aware of the Korean government's role in orchestrating and funding the spread of Hallyu, but he believes that the world's television tastes have been changing for some time and the popularity of K-dramas was almost inevitable. Seung pointed to increasing audience frustration with American prime-time television, which has become so stagnant: "There's only a limited [number of hours in prime time], so studios don't want to take risks," he said—risks such as airing non-American shows.

Bak is certain that the world's interest in non-American programming is not limited to K-dramas. For example, he is betting on a Spanish television drama series called *Isabel*, a costume drama about Queen Isabella I of Castile, perhaps best known for funding Christopher Columbus's journey to the New World. Bak said that *Isabel* was Spain's number one–rated show in 2012, but—he points out emphatically and with disbelief in his voice—*"Not one single U.S. distributor picked up Isabel."* Guess who did pick it up? DramaFever.

Bak feels that American television is losing the future because it has done almost nothing to accommodate to global tastes. Meanwhile, says Bak, "The world loves K-dramas." One reason? "Unlike shows from some other countries, including telenovelas, where characters have sex in the first two minutes, a Korean drama can get to episode eight before the couple has even a slight kiss. The dramas focus a lot on story and courtship, and women all over the world especially want that. In Iran, women schedule their dinners so they don't interfere with their Korean shows. And Africa loves this stuff." Also, Bak notes, third-world countries are accustomed to watching shows with subtitles. They don't really become automatically addicted to any given show just because it's American. Part of Bak's job is to study audience analytics, and he says one trend is undeniable: the United States' monopoly on world television is going out not with a bang, but with a whimper.

## WINTER SONATA: HOW A DRAMA CONVINCED JAPAN THAT KOREAN MEN MAKE GREAT BOYFRIENDS

For years, the unspoken brass ring of Korea's pop culture export strategy was winning over the Japanese audience. If Koreans could melt the hearts of the Japanese—who up until that point had been the dominant pop culture influence in Asia—anything was possible.

Korea's cultural Waterloo was the psychotically popular 2002 dramatic series *Winter Sonata*. This show was the first hard evidence that Korean pop culture could break barriers. *Winter Sonata* became a hit in countries as far-flung as Iraq, Russia, Egypt, and Uzbekistan. But more crucially, it won over Korea's former nemesis from time immemorial, Japan.

When two writers, Yoon Eun-kyung and Kim Eun-hee, first set about writing *Winter Sonata*, they were given two guidelines: the storyline had to have amnesia in it, and it had to take place in winter. Other than that, they had carte blanche.

Laugh all you want; that was all the information they needed to invent one of the most perfect male protagonists in TV history, the amnesiac architect Kang Jun-sang. As a mean girl crushing on Kang in the series rhapsodizes, he has the whole package: "strength, intelligence, and compassion."

The lead actor, the soft-featured Korean actor Bae Yong-joon, became the It boy among Japanese women, and the object of one of the greatest national crushes of all time. Japanese middle-aged women became rabid for both the character and the actor.

The twenty-episode drama aired in Japan in 2003. The obsession grew so large that *The New York Times* took note, covering Bae-mania in a 2004 article tellingly entitled "What's Korean for 'Real Man'? Ask a Japanese Woman."[5] According to the article, *Winter Sonata*—but really, Bae—has been credited with the $2.3 billion rise in new business ventures— across multiple industries, both hard and soft—between Japan and South Korea between 2003 and 2004. Tourism from Japan to Korea increased by 40 percent in the first half of 2004, the same article reported, including trips to the dinky little island where the show is set.

In August 2004, then–prime minister of Japan Junichiro Koizumi said during elections for the upper house of Parliament, "I will make great efforts so that I will be as popular as Yon-sama" (Bae's honorific nickname in Japan).

How did this Bae frenzy get so out of control? For some reason, Japanese women read enormous cultural stereotyping in the physical appearance of one actor. The writers Yoon and Kim were initially bewildered at the success of their show in Japan, though they did offer a few theories as to how it occurred. Kim said, "Japanese women think that Korean men are warm, that you can count on them." Yoon added, "They think Korean men are romantic and protect their women. Bae has a face that does not exist in Japan: manly, yet soft."

*Winter Sonata* is the archetypal Korean drama: it centers around the sanctity of memory, both in the literal sense (as in, someone has amnesia) and the nostalgic sense. It is a world in which the past is somehow more important than the future—not a very New World notion. The plots revolve around childhood innocence, family drama, and a lot of extremely loud crying. Crying, by both men and women, is a big fixture in K-dramas, tapping into Koreans' *han* and their need to fixate on suffering. *Winter Sonata* is less *han*-filled than some Korean dramas, but there are harsh lessons about the uncontrollability of fate and the fixedness of human nature.

*Winter Sonata* starts with the principal characters in high school, when Jun-sang first meets his childhood sweetheart, Yu-jin. Jun-sang has the social awkwardness of Mr. Darcy from *Pride and Prejudice*, avoiding friendships and being brusque with everyone except for one other male student, whom he secretly knows to be his half-brother.

Jun-sang has great hair. He is also a math prodigy. Just as Jun-sang and Yu-jin are about to have a New Year's Eve rendezvous, Jun-sang's mother announces that they are moving to the United States. As in, immediately. As in, that second.

On the way to the airport, Jun-sang is hit by a car. The next day at school, it is announced he is dead.

Obviously, Jun-sang is not really dead or there would be no more episodes. The accident gave him amnesia. In the last five minutes, Jun-sang gets emergency brain surgery, goes blind, and remembers who his high school sweetheart was. They reunite. In the entirety of the series, the main couple only kisses twice, mouths closed.

## CHUNG TAEWON: INVENTOR OF THE KOREAN SPY DRAMA

Given that Koreans live under the constant threat of invasion and nuclear annihilation from the north, it's surprising that Korean television did not have its own spy drama until the popular series *Iris* (2009), about a fictitious Korean black-ops agency that takes on an equally secret terrorist organization named IRIS. The show became a runaway hit all over Asia (apparently, even in North Korea, via bootleg).

Chung Taewon, head of the eponymous Taewon Entertainment, is the creator of *Iris*. He is so exacting in his work that a member of his own staff described Chung's sets as a graveyard of sacked actors. Chung's nickname is "Kim Il-sung"—after the late North Korean dictator. When I met him, though, in April 2013, I was reminded more of Augustus Caesar. And that's what he is—august. He has a round, pensive face full of gravitas and droopy eyes—though the latter feature was surely because he had not slept or eaten properly for months. His walk was stately and regal; even his floor-length down coat draped over him like an imperial cape.

We met at a golf club in the city of Gwacheon, near Seoul, where Chung was in the middle of filming episode 19 of *Iris 2*, a sequel to the first series, which was based on the format of the U.S. series *24*, a cat-and-mouse chase occurring in real time, stretched across the entire season.

Of course, *Iris* has a realistic edge that can't be found elsewhere in the world. After all, South Korea shares a border with the most volatile nation on earth.

"Koreans see [*Iris*] as realistic," Chung said, "and even for foreigners, North Korea is a real threat. We never know what's going to happen tomorrow. The North Koreans are gangsters. They keep threatening the world, not just once in a while but on a weekly basis. Where *Iris 2* starts, South Korea decides it can't respond to North Korean threats. Instead, South Korea wants nuclear weapons so they can be the north's equal."

Whereas the United States and the UK can get away with straight police procedurals in their television shows, the most famous example being *Law and Order*, South Korean audiences want to see a focus on the characters' personal lives. "Korean TV series have to have a love story," said Chung, his mouth pursing in mild disgust. "It has to have a strong, sad, and anxious ending. That's really tough because on the one hand I'm talking about spies, hostages, and fighting, and on the other hand I have to carry on the love story line. That gets tiring for me to write. The Korean television audience is mostly *ajoomas* [middle-aged housewives]. They make the decisions with the remote control. So if I can't get their attention, it's very tough to bring the ratings up."

Despite the success of Korean shows domestically and abroad, Chung feels that there are still a lot of shackles that prevent TV show creators in Korea from exercising full creativity. In a sixty-two-minute show, the network by law can play up to a maximum of thirty-two commercials. Each commercial is fifteen seconds long. The commercials are not interspersed evenly throughout the episode in U.S. fashion, but rather clustered in long stretches of back-to-back ads, which leads to high audience attrition over the course of any given show's airtime.

Furthermore, the network keeps all receipts from advertising and only partially finances programming. For *Iris 2*, for example, the network provided $3 million; the remaining $12 million had to come from outside sources. This meant that Chung had to succumb to the ultimate humiliation: product placements.

"They have product placements on American TV shows, too," I said, trying to make him feel better.

Chung shook his head. "It's not the same thing. On American TV, the product placement is not that obvious." Whereas on *Iris*, the products are glaring and some of them don't make sense within the context of the show. "Kia is one of our biggest sponsors. So all the characters in *Iris* have to drive a Kia. Whether the characters are South Korean, North Korean, or European. We had to send Kia models K5 and K7 by airplane to Hungary so all the actors there would be shown driving it."

He continued, "Our second biggest sponsor was Samsung. Everyone uses Samsung phones, even the North Koreans, even as a spy camera. Also, there is no reason in *Iris* why anyone had to be on a bike, but we had to show a Mando bike—an electric bike—four times over the course of twenty episodes." The root of the problem, said Chung, is that the national television networks are still very powerful and don't invest a lot of money in shows that "don't fit within their rules."

In addition to product placements, Chung had to hustle by selling the *Iris 2* rights overseas before the series was even finished. The gamble paid off: *Iris 2* has been sold to Japan for $6 million, making up over a third of the budget.

To maximize funding, Chung put together a multimedia entertainment extravaganza—typical Korean entertainment company fashion. *Iris* is a video game, as well as a live concert that toured only in Japan.

The *Iris* concert, which aired in 2010, featured the leads of *Iris* singing a song or two—including Lee Byung-hun, who has made a name for himself as an action star in Hollywood films like *GI Joe* and *Red 2*. This was followed by the K-pop boy band Big Bang, singing the song it provided for the soundtrack. There were a few pyrotechnics: a light-and-sound show; a stylized reenactment of a chase scene that evoked *West Side Story* but with some actual, fairly dangerous on-stage stunts; then— perhaps most important—the *Iris* stars expressed their heartfelt thanks to the fans in a mixture of Korean and Japanese. The concert was a smash.

Chung knows better than most how big a deal Hallyu is. Before he became a television producer, he was a concert promoter: first in Los Angeles, then in Seoul. He was responsible for bringing acts like Celine Dion, MC Hammer, and Michael Jackson to Korea for the very first time. In those days, it was an uphill battle getting the artists' agents on board. "People would say, 'Where is Korea?'" Chung recalls.

No one will ever ask him that again.

As Chung demonstrates, Hallyu may be a machine and a national strategy, but history is still made by great men. At the end of the day, the biggest milestones in the export of Korean popular culture are always brought about by individual artists with talent and vision. In K-dramas, the great men (and women) may be the creators of shows like *Winter Sonata* and the *Iris* series. In film, the great men—in my opinion—are director Park Chan-wook (*Oldboy*, *Stoker*) and a mild-mannered civil servant and professor you've never heard of: Kim Dong-ho.

# 11

# K-CINEMA: THE JOURNEY FROM CRAP TO CANNES

· · · · · · · · · · · · · · · ·

LIKE MANY WHO GREW UP IN SEOUL DURING MY TIME, I had no interest in watching Korean movies at the cinema. Until the 1990s, there were only a few genres: cheap and formulaic cop dramas, doomed romances, and moralistic films about vice and addiction. Even the Korean auteur films were overly artsy and not in a good way: very sparse dialogue, no plot, and with bleak and dissatisfying endings. One highly celebrated Korean film released in 1993, *Seo Pyun Jae*, was so torturously boring that given the choice, I'd have preferred to undergo waterboarding, but I couldn't walk out because my father was making me watch it. It was about a little girl training to be a classical Korean singer, but her father feels she doesn't have enough depth of sorrow—specifically, not enough *han*—so he gouges her eyes out. His plan worked; she became a consummate, if blind, singer, so: happy ending. I fell asleep during the film and got yelled at by my dad, who was constantly frustrated in his attempts to make me appreciate

Korean culture. Pointing out to him that my grandmother had fallen asleep as well did not help matters.

Mostly, we'd watch Hollywood blockbusters, French films, or that year's Cannes winners. Seoul only had a handful of theaters, mostly enormous but always crammed. Owing to the disproportionately high ratio of the population to the number of screens, getting tickets to any of them was often an ordeal. Because of a quota limiting the number of foreign films entering the country, theaters would show one film for months and were slow to bring in new films. Moreover, complicated licensing agreements meant that it sometimes took over a year for foreign movies to hit Korean theaters.

The biggest hit of my youth was a French film, the Sophie Marceau vehicle *La Boum*, about a twelve-year-old girl who throws a big party to get the attention of her crush, Mathieu. The film was released in France in 1980 but it took about five years to reach Korea. It was my favorite movie. I loved that the heroine's grandmother was the one who came up with the scheme for capturing Mathieu's heart—something no Korean grandmother would do for her preteen granddaughter—and that a children's film showed a father who has a mistress and it was handled comedically. The movie sparked my lifelong Francophilia.

*La Boum* is just one example of how movies were a means of escape for Koreans. From the Sandra Dee films of my parents' day to the French teen flicks of mine, movies for Koreans were a means of dreaming of a different fantasy life. No wonder we didn't watch Korean films.

Cinema is yet another area in which government intervention in culture paid off in spades. Korea once again demonstrated its unique magic trick: by passing a few new laws and fertilizing the right areas with money, it was able to spur explosive creativity and an entire film renaissance.

In the years following Korean democratization in 1987, the nation relaxed the quotas on foreign films. I was delighted, but the immediate aftereffects of the new openness weren't good for Korea. The government discovered to its horror that its worst nightmare had come true: western pop culture was taking over the country.

In 1994, an article that ran in the South Korean newspaper *JoongAng Daily* reported that ticket receipts for non-Korean films went up from 53 percent of the total in 1987 to a whopping 87 percent in 1994. The Korean film industry was suffering, producing about half the number of films it had made a decade prior.

South Koreans were at a turning point. They could have reacted by banning foreign films, but the horse was already out of the proverbial barn. How can you get him back once he's seen the cyborg policeman turn into liquid metal in *Terminator 2*? Instead, Korea crafted a completely different strategy: beat Hollywood at its own game—or at least try to.

In May 1994, the Presidential Advisory Board on Science and Technology published a report positing that if *Jurassic Park* could make as much money in a single year as selling 1.5 million Hyundai cars (twice the annual sales of that car), then South Korea should be making blockbuster movies, too. The government acted swiftly, removing censorship restrictions and creating tax incentives for companies investing in filmmakers.

In 1995, Kim Young-sam issued a presidential decree—*a presidential decree*—to enact the heady-sounding Promotion of the Motion Pictures Industry Act, which stiffened the penalties for violating the preexisting (but not clearly enforced) quota system. Under the new act, a movie theater that did not show Korean films for at least 146 days per year would have its business license suspended.[1]

Without these draconian measures, there would probably have been no films like the 2004 Cannes Grand Prix–winning revenge film *Oldboy*.

## MR. VENGEANCE: *OLDBOY* DIRECTOR PARK CHAN-WOOK

Park Chan-wook is the kind of writer-director who makes me wish there was a better word than "genius" to describe someone. A word that was not so overused as to be emptied of meaning.

Best known for his so-called vengeance trilogy—*Sympathy for Mr. Vengeance*, *Oldboy*, and *Lady Vengeance*, Park is, in the entire history of cinema, the undisputed master of revenge. He is to revenge what Alfred Hitchcock is to suspense, what Peter Jackson is to fantasy, what Lars von Trier is to anti-American films with shaky camerawork.

Since winning the Cannes Grand Jury Prize for *Oldboy* in 2004, Park has been the most famous director ever to emerge from Korea. Quentin Tarantino, who has often spoken of his admiration of Korean films, is a huge Park fan. While on the

Cannes 2004 jury, Tarantino pushed for *Oldboy* and subsequently played a large part in advocating the film's North American release.

Aside from his Cannes bona fides, Park made the world's first film shot entirely on the iPhone (*Night Fishing*, 2011).

Park did not set out to become a filmmaker—that was not really a viable childhood dream for any Korean from his generation—he was born in 1963. As an undergraduate at Seoul's respected Seogang University, he studied philosophy but his heart wasn't in it once he realized the Catholic-run university's philosophy department offered more courses in Thomas Aquinas than in aesthetics, where his true interest lay. So he started a university cinema club and, upon graduation, wrote film reviews for a living, worked on the occasional film crew, and made a few small films that got little attention.

His big filmmaking breakthrough came in 2000, with the timely and deeply moving feature film *Joint Security Area*—a movie whose tear-jerking political moral would surprise fans who only know Park for his vengeance films. The film tells the fictional story of North and South Korean soldiers serving on either side of the demilitarized zone who accidentally become fast friends, even though the friendship could cost them their lives. At the time, it was the highest-grossing film in Korean cinema history.

Shortly afterward, Park embarked on the vengeance trilogy that made him famous. Park's intensity—the pureness and one-mindedness of the avengers—cut through decades of pretentious Korean films and hypnotized audiences as no

Korean film had before. In Park's films, revenge is beautiful. The avengers become invincibly strong, their senses are sharpened, and they have laser-sharp focus on their target. They are beyond good and evil. Never before had a Korean director so clearly defined what it meant to be an antihero or brought such immediate emotional engagement from audiences.

I asked Park what his fascination with revenge was. He said, "Vengeance is comprised of the most extreme human emotions, when you set out to explore the human condition, it becomes a very interesting experimental environment." Clearly, his philosophy studies continue to inform his work.

In Park's film universe, revenge is not base; it's highly evolved. Park believes that vengeance actually goes against animal instinct; animals try to preserve themselves, whereas humans do not: "Through an act of vengeance, you can't ever actually hope to achieve anything effective or gain any benefit. Because it is very human to be able to invest yourself in something without having any real benefit, without expecting to gain anything."

*Oldboy*, which Park wrote and directed, is a prime example of this. Based on a Japanese manga and loosely on Alexandre Dumas' novel *The Count of Monte Cristo*, *Oldboy* tells the lurid tale of a slovenly everyman, Oh Dae-soo, who is abducted and placed in a highly illegal private prison where rich people hold people they don't like. Oh remains there for fifteen years, where he is served nothing but dumplings.

When Oh is finally released, for reasons as mysterious as his imprisonment, he is importuned by a smelly homeless man who hands him a cell phone and a wallet stuffed with cash. The cell phone rings. Oh answers it. It is his captor, daring Oh to find out what he was being imprisoned for. What ensues is a glorious duet of mutual vengeance between two men, each of whom is simultaneously captor and prey. The violence is gory but also wildly imaginative. No one really dies of gunshot wounds in a Park film. Each act of violence is a ballet. Park not so much frightens you as he captures your own nightmares. You have no idea how chilling a close-up of teeth can be until you have seen a Park film.

Unlike the mainstream vigilante genre, Park's films are not for escape. They are meant as philosophical confrontations, engaging the audience in a debate over honor, loyalty, violence, and the fundamental question of what it means to be human. They force you to confront yourself when, for example, you see a man cutting off his own tongue with a blunt pair of scissors and you catch yourself thinking, "That's exactly what I would have done."

Cathartic though they might be, Park's films offer very little in the way of redemption. When I asked him what he thinks happened to the avenging protagonists after the events of the movie, Park said, "I imagine they would feel quite empty because they have lost their goals and their reason for existence."

Part of the global appeal of the vengeance trilogy is that the audience projects themselves onto the screen and into the avenger's shoes. Park said, "It's no different from a romance film, for example, in that every audience member—and the filmmaker—would like to do something similar to the story portrayed on the screen. In the same way, a revenge story is one that audience members deep down would like to feel themselves."

His comparison of his revenge films to a romance film is a bit of a revelation. Just as one anxiously hopes, in *An Affair to Remember*, that Deborah Kerr and Cary Grant stop missing each other by seconds, so does one hope in *Oldboy* that Oh and his avenger will get to be in the same room.

Park has been making a foray into Hollywood. In 2013, Spike Lee released the American remake of *Oldboy*, and Park himself directed his first English-language film, the noir thriller *Stoker*, starring Nicole Kidman, Mia Wasikowska, and Matthew Goode.

The chief difference Park noted about Hollywood film-making was "how strongly a studio would voice their thoughts to the filmmaker. They have a lot of questions and opinions directed at the filmmaker." In Korea, by contrast, the studio system is much smaller and everyone has pretty much worked with everyone at some point, so Korean directors have more autonomy. Still, Park was so impressed by the American dialectical method that he said he preferred the final studio cut to the director's cut: "In truth, if you compare the movie made with my own ideas compared to the discussions and debates resulting in what you see now, the latter is actually the better version of the film."

Korean films, by contrast, are much smaller projects with fewer staff. Korean directors are also playing with much lower budgets than are their Hollywood counterparts, so the studios are less risk-averse and more likely to give a respected director free reign. When a Korean director makes a movie, it tends to be a reunion of people he has worked with before. The familiarity between director and actor in a Korean film is evident and the synergy is tight—more like a stage play than a film.

Oddly enough, I didn't really discover Korean films until I lived in France—a country that loves cinema, and where Korean films are highly popular. In fact, despite *Oldboy*'s recognition at Cannes and other European film festivals, it did not get a single Oscar nomination, not even for Best Foreign Film. Park believes his appeal in Europe is greater than in the United States because of the finicky nature of the American filmgoer. "In America, only a certain number of people go to a movie with subtitles and appreciate it. Whereas in France, people are more accustomed to seeing movies with subtitles."

Many feel that the subtitle issue will prevent the film aspect of Hallyu from being strongly felt in the United States. On the other hand, some experts believe that movies are Korea's next big export. In the past, Korean producers didn't have enough financing to make a major export push.

Getting U.S. audiences to pay attention to the booming state of K-cinema is a challenge. Culture critic Lee Moonwon said, "Americans think that Korean films are for Koreans. U.S. producers would never think a white audience would watch a Korean film." That said, however, demographic trends suggest that this bias might not be as big an issue in the future. "American distributors think about population ratios," said Lee. "So if the Latino population is increasing, they'll think, 'We should make more movies for Latinos.' Similarly, U.S. distributors are already anticipating that the Asian population will become big enough to require more films catering to that demographic." He added, "Minorities in the U.S. are increasing, so race and language are less significant barriers. The audience for Korean films is obviously going to increase."

The godfather of Korean film, to whom Park and every contemporary Korean filmmaker owes a debt, is not a producer, or a director, or an actor. In fact, when I asked him whether he was a lifelong film fan, he said, "Not exactly."

Rather, the man who pretty much single-handedly created the Korean movie industry from the ground up is a former career government official, Kim Dong-ho, who served as the Korean minister of culture from 1961 to 1988. Now a professor of film at Seoul's Dankook University, and one of Korea's most respected intellectuals, he unknowingly set one of the earliest examples of how the Korean government could create a cultural industry out of whole cloth.

It's not considered politically correct to talk about pedigree in modern-day Korea, but it's significant that Kim comes from an esteemed and genteel background with the highest academic accolades. He graduated from the vaunted Seoul National University, which Koreans annoyingly refer to as the Harvard of Korea. All of which means, to paraphrase a line from *All About Eve*, that nothing from Kim's background or breeding should have brought him any closer to the cinema screen than row E, center.

Until the current generation, Koreans believed that show business in general was not for respectable people. And unlike in the United States, it wasn't at all lucrative, so even the most successful entertainers could hardly say in the face of ridicule that they had cried all the way to the bank. So it took courage for someone like Kim to try to build a Korean film industry, when he could easily have coasted on the guaranteed lifetime security that awaited everyone who passed the difficult civil service exam. But in 1972, he started a five-year plan to promote culture and the arts, and founded Korea's national endowment for the arts. Part of his plan included taking 10 percent of movie box office sales and putting the money toward an art promotion fund. He also built a film studio—Korea had none at the time—in the Korean countryside.

Given that Korea's per capita GDP was $323 in 1972—making the nation poorer than countries like Guatemala and Zimbabwe—bringing about these changes must have been like the Klaus Kinski film *Fitzcarraldo*, in which the title character insists on building an opera house in the Amazon jungle, literally by dragging it there on a rope.

According to Kim, 1998 was the turning point for Korean films entering the international arena. "In the fifty years up to 1997," said Kim, "only four Korean films were screened at the Cannes Film Festival," and even those were screened out of competition. "But in 1998, four Korean films were invited to Cannes."

What brought about that sudden spike? It was the Busan International Film Festival, which Kim founded in 1996. The Cannes program heads saw Korean films in Busan and invited them to Cannes. Since 1998, some four to ten Korean films have been screened at Cannes every year.

In fact, 1998 was a banner year for the Korean film industry, not just artistically but also commercially. It was the year that Koreans started really becoming interested in their own nation's cinema. In 1998, according to Kim, Korean movies constituted only 24 percent of the total market share, with the remainder being almost exclusively Hollywood films. With such local hits as the 1999 spy thriller *Shiri* (starring Kim Yunjin, who played the character Sun in ABC's television series *Lost*) and Park Chan-wook's aforementioned 2000 drama *Joint Security Area*, the market share for local films reached 50 percent for Korean-made films.

This film boom, as with so many of South Korea's pop culture success stories, arose out of a paradoxical combination of constraint and freedom. Once again, the Korean government used its power to boost native industry. Korea had always shown many foreign films, but these all had to be distributed by Korean production companies—of which there were only about twenty until the 1990s. Even then, non-Korean films couldn't just be distributed willy-nilly. Film companies had to produce one Korean movie for every non-Korean movie they imported. It's safe to say that the Korean film industry benefited from this kind of protectionism. France has been doing the same for years; this has allowed its famous film industry to flourish.

Between 1984 and 1987, the motion picture laws were gradually revised and non-Korean film distributors were permitted to distribute their own films in Korea without having to go through a Korean distributor. The timing was not coincidental; 1987 is the year South Korea became a true liberal democracy, and 1988 was the year Seoul hosted the Summer Olympics, forcing Korea's government, industry, and people to be more open to the international business community.

At the time, said Kim, many Korean filmmakers feared that this new openness would wipe them out, that they would be completely crushed by Hollywood blockbusters. Fortunately, this didn't happen, for a number of reasons.

First, the Korean film scene changed fundamentally, partly because many Korean directors and producers started studying their craft in the United States and in Europe, and partly because over the previous two decades, the government gradually lifted its censorship laws. Instead of banning films, the government permitted them with age restrictions, similar to the American G, PG, PG-13, and R ratings. The new freedom gave Korean filmmakers the chance to experiment and push creative boundaries.

Another crucial reason for the surge in the success of Korean films, according to Kim, was that the government gave direct financial support to filmmakers. Incidentally, this is not some uniquely dictatorial Korean intervention; it's a commonality—and a necessity—of virtually every country outside the United States with a successful local film industry. The Korean government created a film council, not unlike that of the UK. Funds were distributed via a grant application system. Kim points out one unusual characteristic: the focus on low-budget and alternative films—quite unlike the Hollywood studio system. The government also built and operated art house theaters.

A third factor in the flowering of Korean cinema is the cultural fund run by the KVIC—the Korean Venture Investment Corporation—a government-backed fund exceeding $1 billion of government and private money, solely devoted to promoting Korean popular culture. As a result of the fund, which was launched in 2005, the film industry no longer had to rely solely on studio financing.

A final factor was the rise of the multiplex. In 2009, the Korean media empire CJ Group launched the world's first so-called 4-D theaters, which are like 3-D theaters with the addition of smell and tactile sensations. For example, when the movie *Avatar* was screened at Korea's 4-D theaters, there was light rain and mist during some of the scenes taking place on the planet Pandora. I'm not sure how many films really need to be shown this way, but it's a totally immersive, otherworldly experience.

Quotas still exist for Korean movies, but at a reduced level. In 1967, a law was instituted requiring all movie theaters to screen Korean films for a minimum of 146 days per year. In 2006, under former president Roh Moo-hyun, the figure was lowered to 73 days. According to Kim, the Korean government compensated by giving the Korean film council a mammoth $400 million check, about half of which came from government coffers and the other half via a mandatory box office contribution. This would be comparable to requiring every American movie theater owner to fund Spike Lee's next film.

That said, however, Kim believes the quotas are now almost a quaint anachronism: "Frankly speaking, this quota has no meaning because now the market share of Korean films has reached 50 to 60 percent. So even if they eliminated the quotas, it would not harm the Korean film industry." Still, the quota system served an important function in creating Korean films until the K-cinema boom of the late 1990s.

I asked Kim why Korean films were so violent. He said, "The top-grossing Korean movies are not violent." He gave three examples: *Miracle in Cell No. 7* (2013), a bittersweet story about a mentally ill man imprisoned on rape charges; *Masquerade* (2012), a historical dramedy starring Byung-hun Lee about a Korean king who dies, forcing his peasant body double to rule the land for fifteen years; and *The Thieves* (2012), an *Ocean's Eleven*–type movie about a heist gone awry.

In fact, on the list of the ten most popular Korean movies, in terms of the number of tickets sold domestically, five are Korean historical dramas or comedies (*The Face-Reader* 2013; *Masquerade*, 2012; *The King and the Clown*, 2005; *Taegukgi*, 2004; *Silmido*, 2003); two are disaster pictures (*Snow Piercer*, 2013, *Tidal Wave*, 2009); one is a heist film (*The Thieves*, 2012); and one is a tearjerker (*Miracle in Cell No. 7*, 2013).[2] At the number one spot is a film in its own genre: a creature feature with social commentary about American imperialism called *The Host* (2006), not to be confused with the American movie of the same name.

Surprisingly, none of the K-horror films or indeed any of

the famous violent Korean thrillers is on the list. Yet gore is what the west expects from Korean cinema. Most of the world is used to getting their rom-coms and police movies from Hollywood, their brooding films from Sweden, their bucolic tearjerkers from Italy, and their mad arty movies from France. Moviegoers in general have a long history of affixing certain genres to certain countries, and for the most part Korea is stuck with the dubious distinction of the horror-and-gore genre.

Kim Dong-ho, who has served Korean cinema mostly behind the scenes in a governmental capacity, is an often unsung hero. But after director Kim Ki-duk won the 2012 Venice Film Festival's top Golden Lion for his mother-son drama *Pietà*, Kim said in an official thank-you speech back in his native Korea, "51 percent of this trophy should go to Kim Dong-ho."

# 12

# HALLYU: THE SHOT HEARD ROUND THE WORLD

. . . . . . . . . . . . . . . . .

HOW SERIOUSLY IS KOREA TAKING HALLYU WORLD domination? Well, the government and its many agencies have been regularly issuing what one might call playbooks for entering world markets. *The Art of War*, as it were, but for peddling K-culture.

One book that came into my possession, *Hallyu Forever* (available only in Korean), published by a government organization called the Korean Cultural Trade Commission, is a savvy, well-researched guide on how to approach world markets. There's a blurb on each region, explaining the socioeconomic, political, and cultural factors that might make it a good market for Hallyu, and even includes suggestions on what aspects of K-culture would do well there: film, television, food, etc. For example, the chapter on the Arab world points out the importance of keeping Muslim prayer times in mind (to avoid airing Korean TV programs during those moments), as well as detailing the strict sexual mores that would make certain Korean dramas a bad fit for the Arab market.

Hallyu's penetration can be subtle at times. Wi Tack-whan's *Hallyu: K-Pop Ehso K-Culture Roh* (Hallyu: From K-Pop to K-Culture)[1] lists a number of surprising, little ways that Korea is getting the world's attention, such as the popularity of Melona—green ice-cream fruit bars made by the Korean Binggrae corporation—in Argentina. "How does that make sense in a country with plenty of much better fresh fruit?" Wi's book asks. Russia is a huge importer of kimchi ramen, an instant spicy noodle soup in a Styrofoam bowl.

But of course, the model for the spread of Hallyu, the one Koreans hope to repeat everywhere, is in Asia. How cool is Korea in Asia? Well, in a television advertisement for Lipton ice tea that ran in Thailand in 2013, the premise is that a guy trying to impress a girl goes from loser to stud when he drinks Lipton, so much so that he suddenly starts speaking Korean ("I love you") for no reason. The ad's slogan: "Never lose your cool." Basically, Koreans are the Marlboro Men of Asia.

To get perspective on how Koreans are perceived in Asia, I interviewed Chinese American journalist Jeff Yang, the founder of *A Magazine*, the first-ever Asian American glossy magazine (published between 1989 and 2002), the author of a best-selling book on Jackie Chan, and probably the foremost American expert on Asian pop culture. "Hallyu has become the standard, the universal popular consciousness of Asia," he said. He gives an example of something he witnessed on a recent trip to Bangkok: "I was on a subway and realized there was a very large ad for a Thai telecom vendor featuring Girls'

Generation. Korean acts, including Girls' Generation, regularly hit number 1 on the Thai charts, despite not being in the same language."

Asked to explain the tectonic cultural shifts in Asia, Yang said, "You have a shifting away of the locus of aspiration. A decade ago, it was Japan. A decade before that, it was probably the United States. Now, it's Korea's pop aristocracy."

So what is K-pop's appeal in Asia? Basically, according to Yang, Koreanness is itself the appeal; unlike Korea, Japan and China tried to export their culture in a watered-down, pan-Asian form.

I've said this elsewhere, but it always surprises me when people describe Korea as cool, given that I spent most of my life hating being Korean. I asked Yang what Asians found cool about Korea. He summed up the general Asian view of Korea today:

"What's *not* cool about Korea? It's a land of sleek consumer electronics, long-legged and beautiful women, men who combine soulfulness and emotion with muscles and manly good looks."

In my youth, I had generally thought of Korea as a put-upon, victimized country. But, according to Yang, those traits are part of Korea's appeal to Asia. Because basically, Korea has never invaded anyone.

"I think there's a geopolitical thing going on here," said Yang. "Other countries that have had a pan-Asian influence have also been bad political actors. China and Japan were imperial powers in the past and were perceived as colonialist, or at least big-footed, in the region."

Korea, by contrast, has followed a different path: conquering through its consumer products, not by its might. "Just a generation ago, Korea was an emerging market. [Now, however], people think of Korea as Santa Claus. In Asia, people think, '[Koreans] are the ones who bring that cool consumer stuff into our market.' Koreans are not thought of as economic occupiers—buying up natural resources or acquiring monuments, or otherwise stepping heavily into the culture."

Yang shares the belief expressed by many experts that Korean cool originated with electronics. And Samsung and LG in particular made a strategically crucial move: going after the low end of the market. Samsung, for example, released cheap phones for less affluent nations; Apple has made no cheap equivalent of the iPhone. Yang elaborates, "Samsung and LG were making refrigerators and dishwashers that had enough of a design sense that people could pull themselves into the middle class." In other words, Korean consumer goods became a symbol of hope and upward mobility. "In a cultural unconscious sense, the striving markets of Asia see Korea more as the sibling who made good, as opposed to a godfather, which helps."

Yang does not pretend that K-pop is particularly groundbreaking in and of itself. In fact, its lack of eccentricity is part of the appeal. K-pop is not producing the Mick Jaggers or David Bowies of the world, said Yang. Rather, "Korea has done a great job of standardization. It's provided a package of entertainment and entertainers who are sexy but safe. Adult yet not out of reach."

In other words, K-pop's appeal is only partly about music.

"When people buy into K-pop, they buy into a lifestyle. K-pop is pop culture as lifestyle brand."

Hallyu is greater than the sum of its parts. In fact, the parts are not even sold separately, in a manner of speaking. Korea is a carefully wrapped package deal, whether the consumer realizes it or not. And that may be why Korea has a chance to export its pop culture to the west. As Yang said, "I don't think anyone has ever tried before to make an integrated blend encompassing everything from consumer technology—the hardware, if you will—to the music, videos, and online content. It's an all-out attack on foreign shores."

Yang expressed cautious optimism as to whether Hallyu has a good chance of conquering the west. "It will be interesting to see how it plays," he said. "A generation ago, I would have said that it was impossible. Japan and Hong Kong didn't succeed, why should Korea succeed? But we're facing a different world now. The K-pop engine is creating choices. It's Asian pop culture coming to the west on its own terms, in a nondefensive, nonapologetic, and noncondescending fashion. For the current generation, the global generation, the foreign is aspirational."

## HOW JAPAN LOST THE CULTURE WARS

If, as Yang said, the locus of pop culture in Asia shifted from Japan to Korea in the last ten years, how did Japan lose the throne?

Japan's pop culture dominance is hurting, and not just in

music. Sanrio, the Japanese company that invented Hello Kitty, had a sales slump from 1999 to 2010 and is trying to bring in new characters to reduce its reliance on Hello Kitty. The Japanese film industry suffered greatly from the decline of anime. As for the once dominant video gaming industry— well, it's not a good sign when one of Japan's top game designers (Keiji Inafune, creator of *Mega Man*) announces, "Our game industry is finished."[2]

South Korea is ready to rush in where Japan now fears to tread. Japan lost its place as cultural tastemaker in Asia, about ten or fifteen years ago. There are a number of reasons for this. First of all, Japanese pop culture, like the Japanese archipelago itself, is too isolated from the rest of the world to have remained a sustainable global influence. This is evidenced by the phrase Japan Galapagos syndrome—coined by the Japanese themselves—which compares Japan's cell phone market to the South American island that has its own species and ecology. In 2010, Japanese electronics company Sharp launched a tablet in Japan that was initially sold nowhere else in the world, appropriately called the Galapagos tablet. Similarly, many of Japan's video games are for the Japanese market only.

Some say the problem is Japan's reluctance to learn English; they're an island nation, and like many countries with a long history of colonialism, they still have a sense that other people should try harder to learn their language. J-pop bands don't strategically include non-Japanese members, for example.

Others, like pop culture critic Lee Moon-won, point out that Japan is a big enough consumer market as it is (the population is 100 million) and is less dependent than Korea is on foreign exports. For many Japanese companies, it's not worth the huge risk of a very, very costly overseas marketing campaign.

It's not just their large population that makes Japan an independently robust market. The Japanese consume a lot, in general. They like new things. On the streets of Tokyo's residential areas, it's not uncommon to see large piles of consumer electronics left at the curb, in perfectly good condition—televisions, DVD players, stereos—because a family has moved and they want to buy all new stuff, rather than take their old electronics with them.

Korea, by contrast, has less than half the population of Japan. Thus, says Lee, Korea had to rely on the export market, "which means they had to pay attention to international tastes to make music that would have global appeal."

Previously, however, K-pop had no international distribution channels. "In order to spread music, you have to have about twenty people pounding the pavement and visiting American radio stations with vinyl records. The Korean music industry had no way of doing that." Only with the advent of the Internet and YouTube was Korea able to break the distribution barrier.

By contrast, in the words of a *Japan Today* article, "Unlike their Korean pop equivalents, most Japanese labels are allergic to promoting their artists' work abroad."[3]

Another reason behind K-pop's overtaking J-pop in the west is that Korean culture is naturally puritanical and conservative, and that's a good thing for global audiences. Despite what you see in Korean movies, sexual puritanism in every-day South Korea is enforced to an annoying degree. A female Korean American friend of mind recalls not being allowed to attend slumber parties as a child, because "You don't sleep at another person's house until you are married." Korea made it easier for other countries to accept their music by emphasizing a buttoned-down image and morals. The general theme of overprotectiveness is an appealing one.

Japan is a different story. It, too, is sexually repressed, but it's not puritanical. Take the J-pop girl band AKB48, so named because the band has forty-eight members. It is currently the most successful J-pop band in Japan. Band members frequently wear school uniforms while performing, and their songs have lyrics like "My school uniform is getting in the way." A song like that would unequivocally be banned in Korea. Not to mention that in Korea, schoolgirl uniforms are only worn . . . for school.

Shin Hyung-kwan, general manager of the Korean pop music channel MNET, explained the band's marketing strategy. "The market for AKB48 is men aged thirty to forty years old. In Japan, there is a culture of selling videos of young girls. The Lolita complex is a phenomenon there." That said, Shin acknowledges that the Japanese music scene is very diverse, much more so than the Korean music scene. "Japan is the world's largest music market, so there is a lot of variety: reggae, ska, etc. But the most profitable is stuff like AKB48."

J-pop bands have a different raison d'être from K-pop bands, according to Shin. "They're there to model and do films. If you look at it from a music point of view, it doesn't make sense. If I look at these bands, there are people who can't sing; some can dance but most can't." Korea, by contrast, is very conservative, which is in fact a conscious K-pop strategy. When they're in markets that like a little more skin, such as the west, Japan, and the more liberal Asian countries, they dress differently.

Lee Moon-won pointed out that in Korea, "there's no one like Britney Spears with a slut image." K-pop bands have to be mindful of their child fans. An inappropriate photo spread or a drug or sex scandal is a career killer. The record label has the right to drop them if something like this happens. K-pop places a great deal of emphasis on boy bands, capitalizing on a long-held Asian stereotype that Korean men are romantic and attentive. The K-pop boy acts (Rain, Super Junior, Big Bang) were popular exports in Asia before the girl bands ever were.

Lastly, it's hard for Japan to compete with Korea in the global pop culture scene, when Japan itself has embraced Hallyu. The Korean music industry realized early on how important the Japanese music market was going to become— despite the nation's historic lack of interest in non-Japanese Asian music. It's also remarkable in light of the fact that overall global music sales are way down, thanks in part to piracy and to the many music subscription services that allow consumers to play thousands of songs for $10 a month.

Key to its success in the Japanese market was having Korean bands record some of their songs in Japanese—in some cases, only in Japanese. It seems like an obvious choice, yet no other country's music industry besides Korea has made a serious effort to meet Japan on its own linguistic turf.

It was a good investment, because Japan's music market has been booming. In fact, in 2012, Japan overtook the United States in domestic CD and online music sales.[4] Japan saw $4.3 billion worth of sales in this area, as opposed to $4.1 billion in the United States—which is a big deal, considering that Japan's population is just over a third of the U.S. population.

A big reason behind robust sales is that Japanese people still buy CDs. CD sales make up 80 percent of Japanese record sales, and digital music downloads actually dropped by 25 percent in 2012.[5] As Bill Werde, *Billboard* editorial director, explained in an interview with Bloomberg, "[The Japanese] love packaging. You can't even buy a little trinket in a Japanese store without having it neatly wrapped and folded and handed to you. I think there's something cultural in the want to have this sort of CD booklet and the album art."[6]

Guess who's been studying the Japanese market for years and is on top of the Japanese love for packaging? Strangely, this is one of those situations in which it frankly helps that Korea was formerly colonized by Japan—Koreans understand how the Japanese think. I remember that my grandparents, and others in their generation who lived under Japanese colonial rule, wrapped things in *furoshiki*—a Japanese silk cloth used to neatly wrap everything from gifts to your own daily lunchbox.

Koreans have been using a variation of *furoshiki* to package their CDs. The CD of Brown Eyed Girls' "Cleansing Cream" album comes with a forty-page photobook, a twelve-page calendar, four postcards printed with members' signatures, and a folded poster, all neatly packaged in a lavender hard case, going for 12,800 yen (around $120) on Amazon .co.jp. The Big Bang "Special Edition" album weighed just over a pound and included a hundred-page photobook. The real wow factor was that the CD opens like the DVD drive of a computer; it slides open automatically if you lay the album flat and press a button. For all these extras, the CD costs around 7,000 yen (about $70). More typically, a K-pop CD with fewer bells and whistles will run from $20 to $40, which is still quite expensive. And yet the Japanese buy them. In droves.

Japanese pop now seems like a distant memory, especially since the Japanese seem to have given up even on their own turf. For the last three years, K-pop bands have swept all the major categories at the Japan Gold Disk Awards—based on music sales and downloads.

## VIVE LE HALLYU: THE SECRET BEHIND K-POP'S SUCCESS IN FRANCE

Korean pop culture's biggest fan in western Europe is one of the few countries in the world with a sense of exceptionalism equal to its own: France.

In April 2011—over a year before "Gangnam Style" appeared—tickets for a multiband K-pop concert in Paris sold out in less than fifteen minutes. There was only one concert date scheduled for the six-thousand-seat arena Le Zénith, featuring K-pop's super elite groups, all from the SM Entertainment record label: Girls' Generation, TVXQ!, Shinee, f(x), and Super Junior. Within days, hundreds of Parisians did a flash mob protest in front of the Louvre to demand additional concert dates. Parallel flash mobs appeared in *eleven other French cities*, including Lyon and Strasbourg. The story was covered by the Korean press as well as the French press, including the daily *Le Monde*.

If you think that the eleven-city flash mob was a spontaneous show of support for K-pop in France, you have not been paying attention. For here, too, there was an invisible hand behind the K-pop machine: as always, a close cooperation between the Korean government and private enterprise. Even the appearance of the media was due to a tip from a Korean civil servant.

I interviewed the man in question—Choe Junho, a theater director by trade and now a professor at the prestigious Korean National University of Arts. He was director of the Korean Culture Centre in Paris from 2007 to 2011—an organization sponsored by the Korean government, devoted to disseminating Korean culture abroad. The Paris branch was founded in 1980 and was one of only three such centers in the world (now there are about twenty-five, according to Choe). When Choe took the helm, Hallyu was already taking hold in France. Under his reign, Hallyu in France became a legend.

The rise of Hallyu was due in part to the popularity of

Korean films like Park Chan-wook's *Oldboy* (2003) and Bong Joon-ho's *The Host* (2006), the latter of which was hailed by France's top news sources—including *Le Monde*—as the best film of the year.[7] Choe, in his capacity as director of the Korean Culture Centre, worked tirelessly to blast France with Korean culture—largely with the assistance of Korean government funds. In the winter of 2003–2004 he screened eighty-five Korean films at the Centre Pompidou, Paris's modern art museum.

It's a reciprocation of interest since Koreans have been diehard fans of French literature and culture for ages. Koreans love the raw emotions and irrationality of French literature far more than they do the social satires and comedies of manners they associate with British fiction.

Victor Hugo's *Les Misérables* was required reading in Korean schools, as was Alphonse Daudet's short story, "La Dernière Classe," for both my parents' and my generation. Set in the Alsace in 1870 or 1871, around the time of the Franco-Prussian war, Daudet's story features a schoolteacher, Monsieur Hamel, who announces that it is to be his last day teaching, because all the French staff are to be replaced by Germans. His last lesson of the class is to impress on them the beauty of the French language. He tells the class, at great personal risk, that as long as you keep your language, you will never be a slave.

Koreans love this story, largely because it's exactly what many Koreans felt when the Japanese colonized Korea in 1910 and banned the teaching of Korean in public schools.

Thanks to Hallyu, the western countries with whom Korea has felt kinship are starting to find the feeling is mutual.

Choe is wholly French-seeming in his demeanor and flaw-less in his mastery of the language, but he still possesses that Korean knack for marketing. In the summer of 2009, he cre-ated a nonprofit, the Korean Connection, which brought to-gether eager French disciples. According to the French daily *Le Figaro*, the group has one hundred thousand members. In October 2010, Choe asked the group what Korean cultural event they would most like to see in Paris. They overwhelm-ingly responded that they wanted a K-pop concert.

Knowing that 2011 was to be his final year at the Korean Culture Centre, Choe wanted to go out with a bang and leave Paris with a taste of Korea it would not soon forget. He approached the Korean Ministry of Culture to request funds for a K-pop concert in Paris in June 2011. "The ministry said they had no money for it; I told them, 'If we do this concert in Paris, you will see Hallyu really take off in Europe.'" The ministry was able to give Choe about 250,000 euros, but it wasn't enough to cover expenses like enticing Korea's top tal-ent and renting out a concert venue.

Choe then approached the Korean megalabel SM Enter-tainment to ask them to put up funds for a giant concert in Paris featuring their own acts. They stalled for a month, said Choe, "because they didn't want to do a project in coopera-tion with the Korean government, and they thought it would not be profitable for them." After Choe promised not to in-terfere in any way with the production or creative vision of the concert, SM agreed to put on the show. On April 26, 2011, the ticket agent Live Nation put the tickets online at

10:00 a.m.; they were sold out in fifteen minutes; this led to illegal scalping, with some tickets going for 1,500 euros.

Choe was determined to get SM to stage another concert. He came up with the idea of staging multicity flash mobs, and used his young French allies at the Korean Connection to help. In order to achieve the maximum impact he had to make the whole thing appear as though it was spontaneous. He contacted the local journalists for the Korean networks KBS, MBC, and SBS and tipped them off that something interesting might be happening on Sunday at 3:00 p.m. in front of the Louvre's giant glass pyramid.

Choe coached his French moles for the camera. "I gave them tactics," he recalled. "I said, for KBS, get a French person who speaks Korean [to approach the camera], for MBC, get someone who sings [K-pop songs], for SBS, get someone who dances. If it was the same for all the channels, it wouldn't be interesting." Choe had expected only fifty to show up at the Louvre; instead, there were between three hundred and a thousand (accounts vary). They broke out into a group dance to some of SM Entertainment's biggest hits, such as the Super Junior song "Sorry Sorry." They shouted their demand in unison, *"Une deuxième date de concert à Paris!"* One more concert date in Paris!

Once the Korean networks started airing the flash mob footage, SM realized they had been beat; they arranged for a second concert. But Choe was not done. He encouraged the Korean Connection to greet the K-pop stars as they arrived at the Paris airport. To his surprise, thousands of fans showed up. "The police said it was the biggest crowd they'd seen at Charles de Gaulle—they lost count." Like many other Hallyu success stories, this one was brought about by a harmonious effort of government, industry, and fans.

Per his promise to SM Entertainment, Choe stepped aside and let it have full creative control. So successful was Choe's disappearing act, in fact, that the French daily *Le Monde* claimed in its laudatory coverage that the concert was the brainchild of SM Entertainment's chairman Lee Soo-man. "The Korean Wave Conquers Europe," read the headline.[8]

"This is the first time I have talked about [my involvement] with a reporter," said Choe. "We used the budget from SM Entertainment very well. We used it to get press; we didn't pocket it." It was the gift that kept on giving; both the supply side and demand side became aware of each other. This opened the floodgates for K-pop stars to book in Paris; no more need to cajole the record label.

# 13

# KOREA'S SECRET WEAPON: VIDEO GAMES

. . . . . . . . . . . . . . .

WHEN I WAS AT SCHOOL IN KOREA IN THE LATE 1980S, students up to high school age were banned from entering video game arcades, at least during the academic year. Which of course meant that I went anyway. It was the schools that enforced the ban; teachers would rotate responsibility for raiding the neighborhood arcades and kicking students out. Video games were considered a corruptor of youth, or we were supposed to be studying instead—something along those lines. The arcades were nothing to write home about. They were in dingy, windowless, poorly lit rooms and run by thugs, as one would expect from a semi-underground industry. Most of the games were from the United States and Japan, they were several years behind the times, and there weren't that many of them to begin with. They didn't usually have marquee games like *Pac-Man*; they were mostly fixed shooter games like *Galaga*. They were never really that popular.

Consequently, Korean video games took a long time to get off the ground. All content industries—games, books, comics, movies, songs—were tightly regulated by the government, which made it hard to import games from abroad. It was also not the best incentive for Koreans to develop their own games.

Fast-forward to 1998. It's the height of the Asian financial crisis. Unemployment levels have doubled. One of the few industries that are booming is PC rooms—what Koreans call Internet cafés. They are full to bursting, but not with happy kids; rather, with humiliated, unemployed businessmen and women having to kill time on the Internet all day long. Little did these unemployed executives know that their sad hours spent procrastinating and evading reality would give rise to one of Korea's biggest cash cows.

It was the unemployment crisis that gave birth to the Korean video game industry, now the second-largest in the world after China's.

At first, the unemployed spent their days at PC rooms looking for jobs and printing their CVs—as well as avoiding the pitying eyes of their families. To while away the time, they started to play video games. Their heavy gaming use did not go unnoticed. In fact, it became an important component of a perfect storm, for at that moment, the country was trying to find new industries to focus on.

In the throes of the Asian financial crisis, President Kim Dae-jung declared that Korea would become the most technologically advanced country in the world. It might sound kind of counterintuitive to announce, in the middle of financial turmoil, that you are about to spend an enormous amount of money on infrastructure, but Kim saw that technology was the way forward.

Once again, government and industry joined forces to create the online gaming industry. Kim significantly increased venture capital for computer hardware and online networks and created tax incentives for software start-ups, including video game designers.

Korea's Internet culture at that point was already very powerful. Kim's government started investing more money to create an even faster, more far-reaching Internet. Private ventures banked on the Internet as well. At this point, according to Kim Sung-kon, who works for the gaming industry lobby group KAOGI (Korean Association of Gaming Industry), the final component of the video gaming ecosystem came into play: "Game developers started to create more games to leverage the expanding infrastructure. So the network, games, and content came together all at the same time." It was a self-perpetuating beast.

A ready audience was waiting. Gaming was already a popular pastime in Korea by that point; in fact, in 1996, the Korean video game company Nexus released what it claimed was the world's first MMORPG—massively multiplayer online role-playing game—though the United States released several games at around the same time. The game, called *The Kingdom of the Winds*, was based on a graphic novel about a fantasy version of ancient Korea (an English-language version of the game was released in 1998). But, as with all Korean products, focusing on just the local market was not a good long-term strategy; with a population of only 50 million, Koreans could only buy so many games. So the gaming industry and the Korean government focused on exports.

Korean-made video games now constitute a quarter of the world market. Even most Koreans have no idea how big Korea's gaming industry. As Kim told me, "In a [Korean] quiz show, one of the questions was, 'What is Korea's biggest cultural export?' It was a multiple choice between films, K-pop, video games, etc. The correct answer was 'video games,' and everyone was shocked." Korean video game exports bring in 1200 percent more revenue for the country than does K-pop. In fact, online games account for 58 percent of Korea's pop culture export revenue (official term: the content industry): about $2.38 billion in revenue in 2012, out of a total of just over $4.8 billion.[1]

One of the more popular Korean-made games in the west is the free, online role-playing *Maple Game*. If you've never heard of it and are wondering why you can't think of a single Korean-made video game, it's because Korean video games are exported primarily to China, Japan, and Southeast Asia. What about America and Europe?

"Those are key markets, but they're also console countries," Kim said, meaning most of their playing is on consoles like Xbox, PlayStation, and Nintendo—produced in Japan and the United States—rather than on PCs. Korean game developers have focused almost exclusively on PC-based games: a peculiar gap, indicative of cultural and commercial phenomena. Partly, it was due to history: "Most of the [coin-operated] arcade games in Korea were imported from Japanese companies like Sega," Kim said. "If Korea had developed its own arcade games, there would have been great potential for it to enter the console market."

Korea's reputation for illegally copying games discouraged console manufacturers from entering the market, said Kim. By contrast, online games come from central servers, so piracy is a nonissue.

There is also an amusing cultural reason for preferring PC online games to console, said Kim: "Console games are the kind of thing you're supposed to play in your living room with the whole family. In Korea, parents don't play games with their kids." Part of the reason Korean online games have not made it to the west, he said, is that in addition to their preference for consoles, Westerners prefer to geek out alone in the privacy of their homes. Furthermore, he adds, Europe doesn't have enough high-speed infrastructure to make a huge move from console to PC games. What Europe does have is a powerful mobile network, which is significant, since many industry experts are banking on phone games becoming big in the future. Part of the reason for the surge in phone gaming, said Kim, is that it appeals to older people who didn't grow up playing video games: "Online games are hard, so adults don't want to make the effort. Mobile games are very easy, so there is less of a generation gap with mobile games."

That said, certain cultures have their own distinct gaming preferences. Korean games, for example, are a slightly different species than their Japanese or American counterparts. Korean games tend to focus on plot rather than graphics, whereas American and Japanese games have hyperreal details like individual hairs and the infamous jiggle of female characters' bosoms. Also, Kim said, "Koreans prefer team games. They'll say, 'You be the healer, I'll be the fighter.'"

Korea's close study of its export countries—particularly Japan—makes it easier for Korean companies to market and sell games to fit the tastes of the niche market. Case in point: most of Korea's top video game companies devote a subdivision to developing games in the Japanese language for the Japanese market. U.S. game manufacturers like Blizzard Entertainment or EA don't do that. This might be one of the reasons why games that are top sellers everywhere else in the world—*Grand Theft Auto*, *Call of Duty*, *Halo*—are not even in the top thirty in Japan.[2]

South Korea is the world's biggest manufacturer of free MMORPGs in the world. In this format (*World of Warcraft* is a popular American example), people can play with tens of thousands of people around the world simultaneously—forming teams with them or combating them. As with a smart drug dealer, the game maker's strategy is to make the first hit free. It's when the players want to buy more tools for their avatar (a sword, a gun, virtual money), or advance to higher levels in the game, that the game makers start asking for credit card numbers.

South Korean game makers make it easy for the proliferation of MMORPGs by putting game servers all over the world. Many U.S. game manufacturers don't do this; there is no server in Japan for Blizzard's *World of Warcraft*. This doesn't make it impossible for Japanese to play, but it does make it a good deal more difficult.

According to Kim, the gaps in technology throughout different countries are gradually decreasing as nations catch up to one another, so people won't have to choose what games to play based on their local technology. This is good news for Korean game manufacturers, whose emphasis on story rather than graphics will benefit from this change.

One major limitation to the industry's growth starts at home, with the Korean Youth Protection Act. While the government does not ban games outright, they give adults-only rating to a lot of games that, in other countries, children have easy access to. Excessive violence or sex is a common basis for a clampdown. As a result, many games aren't widely available, and game designers leave Korea to create games in more tolerant markets. "Only Germany and a few other countries have youth protection laws. Korea's is one of the strongest. I think it's because of Confucianism. [The Youth Protection Act] is basically a parents' rights law," comments Kim. In recent years, the Korean government has cracked down on video games far more than on other entertainment genres, like film. President Lee Myung-bak (2004–2008) clamped down hard on the Internet and on game content in particular. His legacy continues. The game *Homefront*, released in 2011, in which players fight against a North Korean occupation of the United States, was banned because it was deemed too politically explosive. The re-release of the fighting game *Mortal Kombat* was banned in 2011 on grounds of extreme violence.

Kim thinks the prudishness also has to do with pressure from Korea's Christian leaders—Lee was the most openly practicing Christian president in Korean history. He strongly enforced the youth protection laws. But the situation might be looking up. Kim said, "The current president, Park Geun-hye, is facing something like the IMF situation. [This is what Koreans call the Asian financial crisis.] The economy is bad, there's a lot of unemployment. It's quite a similar situation. Now Park's slogan is the 'creative economy,' so they're creating incentives and an environment for new technology that will foster creativity."

The Korean gaming industry has come under fire, domestically and internationally, following widespread reports of Korean Internet addiction. In 2005, a twenty-eight-year-old Korean man died after playing *StarCraft 2* for fifty straight hours in an Internet café. Another incident heard round the world took place in 2009, when a Seoul couple neglected their baby daughter, who starved to death because they were spending all their time at an Internet café playing an online game called *Prius*.

Kim thinks that the game industry is being unfairly blamed for what is really an underlying Korean ailment. "Korea's development has been very condensed, so the society as a whole has high stress. Students are very stressed, adults have to make money fast, and when the government makes policies, there have to be results right away. The biggest problem in such a condensed atmosphere is unhappiness. Korea has the highest suicide rate in the OECD. Everyone is blaming everyone. So the game industry is the scapegoat."

The press usually overlooks gaming in its coverage of

Hallyu, and of all the forms of Korean-produced pop culture, gaming bears the faintest Korean stamp. But government number crunchers know that gaming is leading the wave. And unlike K-pop music, for example, the video game industry creates new jobs for all sorts of ordinary citizens—software developers and even professional players, not just a select few superstar performers.

## STARCRAFT 2

A Korean cottage industry on its own is Blizzard Entertainment's real-time strategy (RTS) video game *StarCraft 2*. The world's top ten players are all Korean, even though the game is U.S.-made.[3] At the time of its 2010 release, the game, which involves combat between humans and alien forces with supernatural powers, was the fastest-selling role-playing video game in history: some 3 million copies were sold in its first month on the shelves. There are currently fewer than half a million active members, but there are 3.4 million teams, suggesting that many players serve on multiple teams.[4]

One of Korea's most famous *StarCraft 2* figures is the director of the Global StarCraft 2 League, Chae Jung-won. Chae hosts the GSL games on GOMTV, a streaming television network based in Korea. Four to five days a week, for four to five hours a day, Chae's show broadcasts live tournaments, in real time, with Korean and English simulcasts. The matches culminate in a world championship four times a year, with a $50,000 cash prize for the winner. All players have corporate sponsorship. And, according to Chae, the championship finals have as many as half a million viewers worldwide (a high number for a streaming broadcast), of which 70 percent are outside Korea.

It is now possible in Korea to make a living in e-sports (video game tournaments); Korea has five television channels devoted to gaming twenty-four hours a day; the United States only has one well-known gaming channel, G4. Chae is emblematic of the vast changes in Korean culture in recent years: he studied to be a geneticist but has abandoned that plan. However, he's semiretired as a player and focuses on his career as gaming channel host. "Video gamers are like professional athletes," he told me. "You can't do it forever."

When I asked why *StarCraft 2* in particular was so popular in Korea, he said, "The game ends quickly, so you can start a new one," echoing one of the traits for which Koreans are best known—impatience. "Koreans like games that are fast and they like to compete."

Furthermore, said Chae, *StarCraft 2* is conducive to playing in a social setting, with most playing occurring in Internet cafés, where people can sit alongside all their friends, rather than at home alone—a hallmark of Korean gaming.

Chae is truly a symbol of the millennial generation—not just in Korea, either. He is among the first crop of gamers for whom a lifelong career in e-sports was a viable option. The Korea in which he grew up is nothing like that of my childhood, in which we had to sneak into arcades to play outdated

American and Japanese video games. Fortunately, technology breeds short memories. Once the next gadget comes out, people seem to forget all about the previous one. If it were not for this, Samsung would have been royally screwed.

# 14

# SAMSUNG: THE COMPANY FORMERLY KNOWN AS SAMSUCK

. . . . . . . . . . . . . .

JUST A FEW DECADES AGO, ALMOST EVERY PIECE OF electronics that came out of Samsung factories was a piece of crap. As business professor Chang Sae-jin noted in his book *Sony vs Samsung*, even simple technology like the Samsung-made electric fan "was so poorly designed and manufactured that merely lifting it up with one hand broke its neck."[1] Communist East Germany probably made better electronics than Samsung did. In 1993, Samsung couldn't even convince its own countrymen to buy its cell phones. Samsung ranked a pitiful fourth place in the domestic mobile phone market, and outside Korea, the phones were practically nonexistent. The fact that the world has forgotten this is a testament to how successful Samsung has been in turning around its product quality and rebranding itself from a low-level manufacturer known for cheap microwave ovens to the world's premier producer of smartphones, semiconductors, and LED and plasma 3-D televisions.

As with many of Korea's success stories discussed in this book, Samsung's rise to the world stage is attributable at least in part to two factors: the direct intervention of the Korean government at crucial stages and its willingness to dive into the digitial revolution because it had no choice.

How amazing is Samsung today? Here's one indicator mentioned in chapter 1. Apple iPhones are made with Samsung microchips, even though the two companies are archrivals in the smartphone market, even though they had over fifty simultaneous patent lawsuits against each other in 2012.[2] Why would Apple do this?

According to Dr. Chang Sae-jin, it makes perfect business sense. Apple could, of course, buy chips elsewhere, but "Samsung was the most efficient producer of key components. [Apple] has alternatives. But Samsung was the cheapest and most advanced supplier."

That said, of course, Samsung chips have become a thorny issue for Apple. When Samsung first started selling chips to Apple, it wasn't making products that posed a threat to the iPhone. But, said Chang, "the issue came up when Samsung began to sell its own mobile phones in the same space as Apple. Samsung came up with the Android phone to compete with the Apple iPhone. So Apple got pissed. It's very natural. It's not right or wrong."

Apple was right to be pissed. In 2012, Samsung was number one in smartphone market share: 39.6 percent compared to Apple's 25.1 percent.[3] Samsung is one of Korea's greatest sources of national pride. The company generates about *one-fifth of South Korea's GDP*, and it's the ninth most valuable brand in the world.[4]

Samsung—like all Korean electronics companies—did a 180 in terms of quality in the last two decades. Even as late as 1985, when my family was preparing to move from the United States to Korea, we had so little faith in Korean technology that we bought all new appliances, including a Sony Trinitron TV, to bring with us, even though import duties were spectacularly high, because having a Korean television was not much different from having none at all.

Chang believes 1995 was the year of reckoning for Korean electronics companies wishing to engage in self-criticism. "Goldstar couldn't do anything about [their reputation], so they dropped the name 'Goldstar' and came up with a new brand called LG." As for Samsung, "They did market research and came up with good news: nobody had heard of Samsung." So the name stayed, even as they reinvented themselves, in what has become a textbook case of successful rebranding strategy.

Samsung (which means "three stars") began in 1938 as a Korean-owned fruit and fish company, during the period of Japanese rule. Chang explained that following World War II, some Japanese companies left assets in Korea, which the government had to sell off. Those with government connections got a good price; Samsung was one of these companies.

Then, Samsung was dealt a very lucky card at the beginning of the presidency of Park Chung-hee, who was determined to push Korea's economy out of the dark ages. In

1962, the government chose some established companies, like Samsung and Hyundai, to be a tool and petri dish for economic planning. Here, "tool" means a real company capable of manufacturing, without which Korea had no chance of lifting itself from post–Korean War poverty. The Korean government helped Samsung and the other golden-ticket-winning chaebols by securing foreign loans.

Companies like Samsung couldn't manufacture so much as a paper clip unless they bought machinery from overseas. But Korean companies had no capital, so they had to borrow from Korean banks—which had no money either—so they in turn had to borrow from foreign banks. None of this was going to happen by itself, and foreign banks weren't knocking each other over to invest in Korean companies with no machinery and no money. So President Park had to arrange the loans his government would guarantee (by raising taxes if necessary), which enabled the enterprise to flourish. In 1969, with the new machinery and capital, Samsung started making electronics.

Fortunately for Samsung, Lee Kun-hee, the third son of Samsung founder Lee Byung-chull, took over as chairman of Samsung in 1987. In 1993, he held a conference for hundreds of Samsung executives at a hotel in Frankfurt, Germany, where he delivered a three-day speech, which became known as the Frankfurt Declaration of 1993. There he famously told his staff, "Change everything but your wife and kids."

Lee was fond of highly dramatic gestures. In 1995, when he found out that some of Samsung's new line of cell phones were defective, he paid a visit to the factory that made them in the town of Gumi in south-central Korea to give the workers there a piece of his mind. On the factory floor, he hung a sign printed with the words "Quality is my personality and my self worth!" He made the two thousand factory workers wear paper bands around their heads with the words "Quality Assurance" written on them. Then he had the workers put the factory's entire inventory in a pile—including some hundred thousand mobile phones—and ordered the workers to smash the items with a hammer. Then he *ordered them to set the whole thing ablaze.* It was a $50 million bonfire.

Of course, highly toxic bonfires aren't enough to make a company succeed. As Chang said, "One of the more important factors of Samsung today is that there was a revolution from analog to digital. If Samsung had tried to compete on the analog stage, it would be impossible to catch up with Matsushita or Sony, because in the analog world experience matters. There were several elements of engineering—mechanical and circuitry—in which Samsung was behind."

So Samsung didn't even try to develop its analog technology. Digital technology, on the other hand, was an ideal blank slate. As Chang explained, "In the digital world, if you make an industry-standard chip, they're all the same quality." Obviously, he doesn't mean that anything goes. He explained, "In the digital world, everything is zero and one, so it's presized in terms of reproduction and transmission."

I remember the first time I learned this. I was in high school during the period when CDs were starting to make cassette tapes obsolete. A friend had copied a Paul Simon CD for me, based on a copy he had made for himself, borrowing another friend's original CD. I said, "Isn't this a copy of a copy? Is the sound going to be okay?" My friend laughed and explained condescendingly that I was thinking in terms of that ancient technology called cassette tapes, in which, indeed, if you were to copy a tape that was itself a copy, then the sound would be compromised. "CDs are binary," he said. Seeing I still didn't understand, he said, exasperatedly, "That means all copies are perfect."

All of which means that Samsung didn't have to worry about quality in the same way as in an analog world, because everyone was equal in this new digital world in which you only had to worry about getting your zeros and ones right.

As was often the case in modern Korean history, being behind in the current technology meant the nation could vault ahead in the next. Nonetheless, the digital gamble was not a sure thing. Lee Kun-hee was a visionary, but he wasn't psychic. Luck and timing were on his side. It may be hard to believe now, but in 1995, it still was not obvious that digital would overtake analog to the extent that it has, as quickly as it has.

Analog technology still had strong proponents in the 1990s, especially in the audiovisual world. Samsung digital TVs depended on countries making the switch from analog to digital television, which is why Samsung TVs did not take over world market share until this century. The United States was very reluctant to make the switch, and did not officially do so until June 2009; the UK made the switch in 2012. That kind of change requires a central government mandate that takes quite a long time in most democracies. Radio, for example, continues to be analog. Part of the reluctance came from citizens who felt that it was fascistic for a government to force people to buy all new televisions. Others, particularly fans of vinyl records, believed firmly that zeros and ones could not convey music with the same intensity and feeling as vinyl, which is largely true.

But inexorably the world did go digital. More important for Samsung, it also went mobile. As Chang writes in his book, the Korean government stepped in again with semiprotectionist measures to ensure the success of its native mobile phone industry. In 1996, the Korean government designated code division multiple access (CDMA) as its communication technology, rather than global system for mobile communication (GSM).

Korea's decision not to adopt GSM was a radical one, as GSM is the global standard for mobile communications, with around 80 percent market share worldwide. But it worked: since most non-Korean phones wouldn't work in Korea, this allowed a brief window during which Samsung and other Korean mobile phone manufacturers could get their phones on the Korean market and create brand loyalty. Furthermore, Samsung added bells and whistles to its phones at a rate that far outpaced that of its competitors. One 2008 model Samsung sold in Korea had a movie projector built into the phone, so you could screen movies on a blank wall using your phone.

But there was one pesky problem: Samsung still needed to refashion its brand image. There was a worrisome phrase floating around the business world in the 1990s, the "Korea discount." This term, more politely called the "emerging market discount," meant either that Korean companies were undervalued on the stock exchange or that Korean commercial goods had to be sold at a cut rate in order to be competitive on the global market. Either way, it was a slight: it meant that Korea was falling victim to its old stereotype as a maker of shoddy products with too much corporate turmoil.

Fortunately, Samsung had been building a dream team. In 1996, Lee appointed a former in-house engineer, Yun Jong-yong, as CEO and vice chairman. In 1999, Samsung brought aboard a Korean American business wunderkind, Eric Kim, to head up its global marketing. They were the new faces not just of Samsung, but of the next generation of chaebol: western, scientifically minded, and rebelling against the old-world model of blind corporate allegiance and endless hierarchies.

Lee Charm explained the cultural significance of Lee Kun-hee's radical reforms. In the old days, said Lee, "Samsung was the model of a Confucian-style [company]," meaning that it was run on a strictly hierarchical follow-the-leader policy. "Then came the Lee Kun-hee revolution. Before, to make a decision, twenty-five people had to give approval. Lee Kun-hee [changed all that], saying there would be no more than three levels of decision-making."

Thus, within a span of a few years, Samsung had made a fundamental quality change (bonfire), bet on the right horse (digital technology including semiconductors and mobile phones), and modernized the corporate chain-of-command structure. The final component of rebranding was a matter of spin. Samsung had to shake off the "Korea discount" label. As any schoolchild will tell you, getting rid of nicknames and reputations is no easy task.

Samsung knew it could not rely on its overseas reputation evolving organically over time. For the first time, Samsung had to do a major western press offensive, meaning it had to do something that at the time did not come naturally to Korean companies: rely on an independent public relations firm.

During the Asian financial crisis of 1997, Samsung nearly went bankrupt. It had only a few years' worth of operating cash. In July 1998, CEO Yun and nine other Samsung executives locked themselves up in a hotel and wrote their resignation letters. They made a pact that they would put the letters away for five months, at the end of which they would actually resign if they didn't cut company costs by 30 percent. This pact spurred executives to wade into the unfamiliar waters of aggressive public relations.

Spinning Samsung was not going to be significantly easier

than spinning Korea as a whole. Samsung had not yet released its Galaxy smartphones. To the outside world, it was a second-tier company that was mostly known for manufacturing unsexy individual components like microchips. A western journalist could hardly be blamed for not getting that excited about it.

But all the cajoling and corporate matchmaking paid off. On June 11, 2001, *Forbes'* front-page story was "Look Out, Sony," describing Samsung's ambition at the time. The article was a milestone that would forever change the way Korean companies talked to the western press. Rather than the usual modus operandi of acting like inscrutable gods, the Samsung executives interviewed for the article showed unprecedented frankness: CEO Yun blatantly and strategically admitted Samsung's weaknesses in order to make a larger point: "We were 30 to 40 years behind in the analog age, but in the digital age, the playing field has been leveled." And Eric Kim, Samsung's head of global marketing, made it clear: "We want to beat Sony. . . . Sony has the strongest brand awareness; we want to be stronger than Sony by 2005."[5]

*Forbes* commented, "That sounds off the wall." At the time, most people would have agreed. Sony was known for making high-quality electronics that made people happy: camcorders, televisions, CD players, PlayStations. Sony had invented the transistor radio and the Walkman. It was seemingly unbeatable, an iconic brand. If you were to unwrap a birthday present and see the word "Sony" peeking out from beneath the wrapping, you'd most likely get very excited. It'd be unlikely you'd have felt that way about getting a Samsung memory chip. To challenge Sony seemed like insanity on Samsung's part.

Yet Samsung did beat Sony; in 2002, three years ahead of schedule and just one year after *Forbes* called the idea "off the wall," Samsung's market capitalization exceeded Sony's. By 2005, its market cap of $75 billion was twice that of Sony's.[6] In addition to its mobile phone dominance, it has since 2005 been the world's top manufacturer of flat-screen display panels, televisions, and of course, the backbone of the company, those unassuming microchips.

Samsung wasn't content to rest on its laurels. The Samsung executive suite was more wound up and ambitious than ever before, so much so that on September 19, 2005, *Fortune* stated, "Samsung's VIP Center is home to a uniquely paranoid culture—and that's the way the boss likes it."[7] Paranoid in what way? Well, it is most apparent at the VIP Center, a five-story building in Suwon, an hour south of Seoul, and intentionally separate from the main corporate offices. It's the technology version of Willy Wonka's Chocolate Factory, serving as a laboratory and brain trust where Samsung's ideas are born and developed. *Fortune* described the center as "an invitation-only, round-the-clock assembly line for ideas and profits where Samsung's top researchers, engineers, and designers come to solve their grittiest problems."[8]

"Failure is not an option," the article continues, quoting Kyunghan Jung, a senior manager of the VIP Center: "Vice Chairman Yun stresses that if you relax, if you become complacent, a crisis will find you." Jung adds, "There is a lot of tension here."[9]

And it's not just quality control. Samsung by then had such advanced technology that corporate espionage began to become a realistic concern. In the men's bathroom, according to the article, each urinal has at eye level a picture of one of the planes crashing into the World Trade Center on September 11, 2001. This is meant to serve as a reminder that loose lips sink ships. Needless to say, there's an obvious logic gap here: September 11 didn't occur because of poorly kept secrets. The image is just meant as a scare tactic.

As amazing as Samsung is, its international appeal doesn't derive directly from Hallyu. People who buy Samsung Galaxy phones or flat-screen TVs don't usually think about bands like Big Bang or movies like *Oldboy*. In that sense, Samsung at first glance seems to fall slightly outside the Hallyu pattern. Which is to say, part of the appeal of K-pop is that it's Korean. For Samsung, that's not likely to be the case.

That said, Samsung is a crucial part of the overall Hallyu ecosystem. As culture critic Lee Moon-won opined, "Hallyu started with Samsung." In other words, the popularity of Korean music and movies is hard to separate from the confidence that Samsung created in Korea the Brand. Most countries that have dominated world culture or the pop culture scene were already wealthy by the peak of their influence. Samsung helped buoy the Korean economy, which allowed the government to finance popular culture products; Korean pop culture, in turn, benefits Samsung, which in turn benefits Korea as a nation. And so on.

But going forward, Korea cannot continue to rely so much on any one company for its economic success. That's why the nation is embarking on the next phase of its development—the "creative economy."

# 15

# THE MINISTRY OF FUTURE
# CREATION

• • • • • • • • • • • • • • • •

AFTER BRINGING THE COUNTRY TO THE FOREFRONT
of cutting-edge technology and popular culture, the Korean
government is now taking definite and expensive steps to
ensure that the twenty-first century becomes known as Korea's
Century.

Immediately after President Park Geun-hye took office in
February 2013, she established a brand-new ministry, initially called the Ministry of Future Creation and Science. As
a friend of mine joked, "It sounds like a ministry that will be
created in the future. So they can't ever actually create it."

The name leaves so much to the imagination—some critics say, far too much. Each question leads to more questions.
What will the Ministry of Future Creation and Science be
doing? The mission statement on its official website says, "Science & technology and ICT [are] the key to the creative economy and greater happiness of the public." ICT is a jargony
acronym for information and communication technology.

The sentence requires much unpacking. What exactly is a "creative economy"? It's the official catchphrase of Park's government, and the new ministry's site defines it as follows:

> *The creative asset that combines creative idea, imagination and ICT plays a pivotal role in stimulating start-ups. New growth strategies can be mapped out to create many high-quality jobs through the convergence with existing industries, which in turn leads to the emergence of new markets and industries.*

In plain language, the government is funding the human imagination. Sounds good, but it's still not very clear.

As one skeptic told me, "President Park is under no obligation to explain. It's the future, so it's intangible. If she could explain it, then it wouldn't be intangible anymore. It's like Edison's lab. They don't know what they're looking for."

In a move that clarified nothing, Korea changed the official English name of the ministry in March 2013 to the less cool-sounding Ministry of Science, ICT and Future Planning. Critics were merciless. The op-ed in the April 3, 2013, English-language edition of the *Korea Times*, said, "Ministry of ICT: Give Pay Cut to Who Named It!"[1]

What is the Park government trying to accomplish with this new ministry?

The website outlines the ministry's five main strategies, including "making software and content industries [pop culture products] the core of the Korean economy"—in other words, bringing IT and Hallyu exports to the next level.

Another strategy is "establishing a creative economy ecosystem." The word "ecosystem" sounds natural and organic, but in human activities, ecosystems never arise by themselves. This ministry with the long name is clearly a Korean-style ministry, meaning that it has to exercise some muscle to put the elements of the ecosystem in motion.

Reading between the lines (and based on the government's previously stated agenda), it's clear that the ministry intends to marshal private enterprise to achieve the goals of "greater happiness of the public." The government nudging private industry to cooperate with national goals is a familiar theme, but this time there is a radical new twist: the ministry wants the big companies to help encourage small and medium-sized businesses to succeed. Now, why would any big company want to help its potential competitors, and what sort of government would have the audacity to ask such a favor? Well, if history is any guide, the government may actually force big companies to cooperate either by mandate or by making them an offer they can't refuse—namely, by making it too costly and distressing for big companies *not* to play along.

The country expects no less, and that would have been true regardless of who took office in February 2013. Park faces the thankless, high-pressure task of turning the nation into a combination of Silicon Valley, Hollywood, and Industrial Light & Magic—only better, faster, and more advanced.

For the first time in Korea history—perhaps in any nation's history—the Korean government is putting huge financial and political resources behind something as intangible as "discovery." No guidelines, no maps; just money and faith.

Building a creative economy is not going to be easy. This was not like that time in the 1990s when the Korean government launched an awareness campaign to get people to start standing on the right, walking on the left on the subway escalators. Turning Korea on its head is going to take more convincing than a few weird posters and TV ads asking people to be orderly.

Onerously, Korea still has not managed to wean itself off its reliance on the chaebols—the mega conglomerates like Samsung and Hyundai. True, these companies have clothed and fed the nation since the 1960s, but they are far too powerful, now more than ever: in 2012, the top ten companies in Korea generated over 75 percent of the nation's GDP.[2] If one of these companies fails, the whole nation will fail.

Park's radical break from Korea's past takes on a personal dimension for her. In order for her to fulfill her campaign promises, she has to dismantle the life's work of her own father, President Park Chung-hee, who ruled with an iron fist from 1962 to his assassination in 1979. (His wife, the first lady, was assassinated in 1974, in what was assumed to be a botched attempt on the president.) It was Park Chung-hee who marshaled the government's resources to build the chaebol economy, which increased Korea's per capita by about 1700 percent during his term. Regardless of the bona fides that suffering the assassination of both parents might bestow upon her, President Park Geun-hye is an untested politician and her opponents are all too happy to rub it in.

She faced an immediate crisis and PR fiasco in her first few months in office, when her first selection to lead her new ministry was rejected by the government. In February 2013, Park tapped Korean American businessman Jeong H. Kim for the job. Kim seemed to embody the spirit of the ministry: he was president of Bell Labs. He was a wunderkind entrepreneur. He was completely bilingual in Korean and English. It would have been hard to imagine a better appointee. And yet he pulled out of the running just three weeks after his nomination, when it became clear that the Korean parliament was going to block his appointment. Some members objected that he had been a paid adviser to the CIA in his capacity as engineer.

In a withering op-ed in the March 29, 2013, edition of *The Washington Post* entitled "A Return to South Korea, Thwarted by Nationalism," Kim slammed his critics: "I was slandered. Some, for example, theorized that I was a spy. Family was considered fair game: My wife was accused of being associated with a brothel."[3]

The subtext of this op-ed is clear to many Koreans: Kim fell victim to the persistent mistrust that many old-fashioned Koreans have for diasporic Koreans—especially Korean Americans. Kim knows it, the Korean media knows it, and Korean Americans know it. It's unfortunate and continually surprising. On the one hand, Korea has become quite a welcoming place for foreigners; many westerners visiting Korea share glowing reports about Korean hospitality and how modern the country seems. On the other hand, Koreans raised abroad have a very hard time smoothly transitioning into Korean society. I am no exception.

I was twelve when my family moved to Korea. I didn't

speak more than a few words of Korean because there was a prevailing belief among many immigrants of all national origins that raising children bilingually was psychologically and intellectually damaging: children exposed to multiple languages would feel torn between two or more cultures and have developmental language delays, or so the theory went. That idea has long fallen out of fashion. But in my case, it meant that I spent my first year in Korea looking like a complete idiot, with a very thick American accent that I never managed to shed.

I was teased constantly by children calling me "Yankee," which was slightly amusing, and mimicking my Korean, which was less amusing. I wouldn't say that the kids were openly cruel, but I have never felt more culturally segregated before or since. Mostly, they just looked at me with incomprehension. For a child, that feeling of being dumb and mute is utterly alienating. Language aside, I was simply a misfit. My facial expressions and mannerisms were all wrong; I made intent, direct eye contact with my betters when I should have been sheepishly looking down at my shoes.

When I insisted on transferring to an international high school in the ninth grade so I could prepare to go to a university in the United States, this unleashed a full year of tears and incessant arguments in my family. By all means, go to the United States for graduate school, my parents said; but if you go abroad for undergrad, you can never, ever live in Korea again. It was not an idle threat. Going to an American university would diminish my chances of getting the plum jobs in Korea, possibly impede my entering into a good marriage, and subject me to the pity and condescension of my fellow Koreans. Now, attitudes toward Korean Americans have become more enlightened, which is to say, we are now recognized as a demographic category instead of just a bunch of pathetic souls whose parents had the bad judgment to uproot us. But when I was in school, my desire not to go to a Korean university was viewed as a cowardly and sly attempt to bypass the hellacious Korean university entrance exam.

People like Jeong Kim and me are not without our sympathizers in Korea. President Park certainly championed Kim. On March 4, following Kim's resignation, Park delivered an abject Korean-style apology, meaning that it was no apology at all but rather a thinly veiled, biting condemnation of the members of her government who were standing between her and her potential staff.

Kim's tarring and feathering was a public challenge to Park's authority, and it was the last thing her new ministry needed. She needed allies—and a distraction. Fortunately for her, she had both in the form of Psy. He didn't expressly support her (or any) campaign, but she certainly supported his. They say politics make strange bedfellows, and these two are the strangest.

I would never go so far as to suggest that Park won the presidency because of Psy, but he certainly didn't hurt. In the wake of his success, Park's dream of a creative economy didn't seem so quixotic after all.

On April 13, 2013, two months after Park took office, Psy

debuted his song and video "Gentleman" in a live concert. There he performed what he calls his "arrogant dance"— swaying his hips from side to side while holding his chin in one hand. He borrowed this set of gestures from another K-pop group, Brown Eyed Girls. But he did it all legally, by paying the choreographers for the right to use it.

On that same day, President Park held a meeting at the presidential Blue House to discuss her brand-new, rechristened Ministry of Science, ICT, and Future Planning. During an official speech at this meeting, she praised Psy's video, exulting, "We are living in an environment in which someone might think they could get away with tweaking the dance moves a little and then not paying royalties to the original choreographer. But [Psy] is an exemplary case of acknowledging creative rights in the content and software arena."

Congratulating someone for not committing dance piracy may sound like damning with faint praise. But Park's praise was highly strategic. She realized that Psy's success hammered home the theme of her presidency: he put the "creative" into "creative economy." Furthermore, she wasn't just paying lip service with all that talk about the importance of copyright. For decades, Korea has had a very serious piracy and counterfeiting problem—from illegal song downloads to fake Louis Vuitton bags—which is a serious challenge when it comes to encouraging innovation.

But Park's detractors continued to be unforgiving. The Korean press was riddled with rumors that some of the civil servants appointed to the new ministry were lollygagging, waiting for clear instructions. On May 7, 2013, an article that ran in the website of the publication *Korea IT Times* bore the mocking title, "Future Ministry Public Officials Waiting to Be Assigned Have No Future."[4]

Still, all signs indicate Korea has a fair shot at achieving a more creative economy, though it's hard to imagine that it will fully embrace Silicon Valley mores and culture. I don't think even the hippest of Korean start-ups would tolerate employees dressed in shorts and sandals or coming into work at 11:00 a.m. just because they'd been up working most of the night before.

There are already signs that Korea has become hospitable to start-ups and innovation. The website for the Ministry of Science, ICT, and Future Planning proudly features a few Korean start-ups that qualify as "exemplary cases of creativity and imagination." One of these is ID Incu (deriving from the words "idea incubator"). Its founder, baby-faced twenty-something Kelvin Dongho Kim, is the poster boy for the "creative economy" in several respects. He's young, he uses a western first name, and his company's business plan allows other start-ups to flourish. It offers a product called Open Survey—a combination of software and service for companies to conduct affordable surveys about their potential products, drawing from an enormous survey pool of 240,000 ID users who have consented to answer questionnaires. Normally, if a small or medium-sized company were to commission a survey on that scale, the cost would be prohibitive.

Kim got his big break from a competition sponsored by the giant Korean mobile company SK Telecom. This is precisely what Park's creative economy calls for: big omnipotent businesses nurturing small businesses. The ID Incu offices are cramped and messy, nothing like my dad's stuffy old office, in which every conceivable surface was covered with doilies, every large room had a grandfather clock, and office furniture was oversize and intentionally intimidating.

The success of some recent Korean start-ups suggests that Korean culture is becoming increasingly more tolerant of Korean Americans. Daniel Shin, a Korean American from McLean, Virginia, with a Wharton Business degree, moved to Korea in 2010 to found Ticketmonster, a website that offers discounts on various products, similar to Groupon. Just twenty months after its founding, according to *Inc.* magazine, Ticketmonster had seven hundred employees and $25 million per month in revenue.[5] In 2011, Shin sold Ticketmonster to the Internet coupon site LivingSocial for a reported $380 million.[6] At the time, Shin was twenty-six years old.

Shin had the foresight to see an industry gap in Korea and jump in with Ticketmonster. But he did butt heads with more conservative Korean business types. Shin told *Inc.* magazine that an executive from a large Korean conglomerate had said he would disown a son of his who dropped a successful corporate life to embark on a start-up.[7]

In short, the creative economy may have its fits and starts, but anyone wagering against Korea's ultimate success would be foolhardy. Despite difficulties with what continues to be a conservative and patriarchal culture, drastic changes are already afoot—not just on the business landscape, but in the very fabric of Korean society.

## THE KOREA KIT

Is there something about the Korean success model that can be bottled and sold, just like its K-pop albums and melon bars? Well, Korea is certainly banking on this. Beginning in 2009, the country has stepped up its efforts in "knowledge sharing"—passing on the secrets of its affluence to some thirty-odd developing nations from four continents, from Algeria to Turkey to Bolivia to the Philippines. In other words, Korea is peddling a wealth kit, something like a combination of a self-help book and the Marshall Plan. Korea is offering these countries a neat little package containing funding, nation-building experts, and strategies—the centerpiece of which is the advice that all countries build government-funded research and policy institutes whose sole purpose is to carry the country from third-world to first-world status.

What rewards does Korea reap from this seeming beneficence? Most likely, a great deal. For one thing, the knowledge-sharing initiative guarantees that Korea gets in on the ground floor with emerging markets. By the time these countries get on their feet, they will already have established partnerships with both the Korean government and Korean industry. In other words, these countries will already have been sold on Korea the Brand and will be more likely to buy Korean products. Korea's outreach, coupled with Hallyu—opiate of the masses—is a full-on amphibious attack with a very high probability for success. The Marshall Plan aid strategy worked for the United States after World War II, which is a major reason the twentieth century belonged to America. After the Korean War, American aid took on so many forms—monetary, military, cultural—that my mother's family named their dog Betty after the character from the *Archie* comic strip. None of this seemed weird at the time; most of the world worshiped the United States. And there is no reason to doubt that Korea's plan will have a similar effect on the developing nations it is currently aiding.

But there are a few lessons of Korean success that can, in fact, be replicated. One of these is the need for a government that is unafraid to interfere with private business and its citizens' private lives. A somewhat alarming example of this is the Korean government's decision, under the presidency of Park Chung-hee, to limit the expansion of universities so as to ensure that there would be enough blue-collar workers to populate the nation's factories and keep the boilers running, so to speak. It was draconian and seemingly uncivilized, and no doubt many suffered for it, but it is hard to argue against its efficacy. Even those workers who might have been cheated out of a university education still have a much higher standard of living than they would have with university degrees if the nation continued as a barely inhabitable backwater unable to recover from the Korean War. In fact, their sacrifice was not in the name of some long-term, abstract hope: those workers were able to see the benefits of living in a rapidly growing nation within their own lifetimes. Their salaries and standard of living rose visibly in five-year increments.

In most capitalist countries, private industries would find this level of government intervention intolerable. Not in Korea, though: the Korean government has always run itself like the board of directors of a giant corporation with 50 million employees. Decisions made at the national level, like making Hallyu a top priority and throwing billions of dollars at it, were arrived at after exhaustive market research and with the close, willing cooperation of its private enterprise sector.

Nearly every Korean triumph discussed in this book is attributable to this highly paternalistic, mostly benevolent system of what one might call "voluntary coercion." Korea's recent boom in manufacturing, Samsung's success switching from food to semiconductors, the nation's massive Internet infrastructure, and widespread export of pop culture—all of these aspects of success came about because of the Korean attitude that what's good for the country is good for business and what's good for business is what's good for the individual. Koreans don't see profit as a zero-sum game, to use an economics term—that is, no one party has to profit at the expense of the other; everyone can win.

Ultimately what it boils down to is that even if Koreans disagree with the government, or are resentful of corporate greed, they think of themselves as citizens of a republic in the sense that Plato intended, wherein citizens believe that the well-being of those around you contributes to your own well-being. This idea is very much alive in Korea. That's why every school in the nation follows the same curriculum; that's why school is so difficult. Even the most elitist of Koreans believe that everyone has the right to a quality education. Call it enlightened self-interest, if you like. Koreans know from experience that everyone must rise together, or not at all.

Another important lesson from Korea's success is this apparent paradox: Being number one matters, but being first does not. Almost every area in which Korea achieved dominance occurred in territory that was well covered by other nations. Korea did not invent the semiconductor, the plasma TV, the mobile phone, or refrigerators, and most definitely not pop music. As appealing as it is to have many patents and innovations to one's credit, history is full of inventions that failed because they came to the market too early. Video phoning was technologically possible decades ago, but people weren't yet comfortable with having to change clothes or put on makeup just to make a phone call—that required a little social evolution and change in attitudes about appearing on camera. Apple released the Newton—an early precursor of the iPad—in 1993. But wi-fi didn't really exist yet, nor did 3G networks, and without those, it was difficult to transmit information to and from the device, so the fact that you could carry it around didn't offer much appeal. Only after it became possible to read e-mail and download information instantly on a tablet did the technology start to take off.

It defies common sense, but Korea was able to get ahead in so many areas because it wasn't concerned about being first. It didn't have the means, for one thing. So by default it adopted a strategy similar to that used by Tour de France cyclists, called drafting. In a long race, cyclists may intentionally fall behind the lead riders so as to be shielded from wind resistance by those in front. Cyclists can draft only up to a point—eventually they have to decide when to pull ahead of the others. Korea has always been good at the last-minute photo finish.

At the end of the day, the most important factor in Korea's success is its work ethic. Surpassing a certain threshold of effort is necessary to push a person or a country from being merely very good to being great.

So how does Korea manage the work ethic and maniacal drive to be number one? The underlying national psychology that motivates the country is not a salutary one. I remain convinced that *han*, that culturally specific, millennia-old rage against fate, is a huge motivating force in Koreans' stamina and persistence. But *han* by definition cannot be experienced by non-Koreans. Another motivator is shame: deep, profound shame and self-flagellation for any and all failings, including allowing themselves to be colonized by Japan in 1910, for post–Korean War poverty, for having to take bailout money during the Asian financial crisis of the late 1990s, and for being second-best at anything. These two traits, *han* and shame, are deeply embedded in the collective Korean unconscious. If Korea were a person, it would be diagnosed as a neurotic, with both an inferiority and a superiority complex. It would be difficult for other nations to mimic this kind of complicated spiritual constitution. Nor should anyone want to, really. For one thing, it took five thousand years for Korea to evolve into what it is now, a superachieving, frighteningly ambitious nation with a mighty axe to grind. Frankly, a great deal of Korea's drive comes from trying to outpace its demons of past and present. If Korea manages to stay ahead of demons yet to come, it could mean that it is in fact always going to be occupying some future space—a vanishing point off in the distance. Korea is the future. Welcome to the future.

# NOTES
·······

## INTRODUCTION

1. Andrew Woodman, "South Korea VC: State Subsidies," *Asian Venture Captial Journal*, Oct. 31, 2012, http://www.avcj.com .avcj/analysis/2221157/south-korea-vc-state-subsidies.

2. Jeff Yang, "Future Pop," *Upstart Business Journal*, Mar. 27, 2008, http://upstart.bizjournals.com/executives/features/2008 /03/27/Music-Impresario-Jin-Young-Park.html?page=all.

## 1: BEFORE COOL

1. The results are drastic: between the years 1983 and 2005— a span of just twenty-two years—Korean life expectancy increased 60 percent for males and 48 percent for females. S. Yang et al., "Understanding the Rapid Increase in Life Expectancy in South Korea," *American Journal of Public Health*, May 2010, cited at http://www.ncbi.nlm.nih.gov/pubmed/20299661.

## 3: THE DYING ART OF SCHOOL THRASHINGS

1. *Republic of Korea: Country Report*, Global Initiative to End All Corporal Punishment of Children, Mar. 2013, http://www.endcorporalpunishment.org/pages/progress/reports/rep-korea.html.

2. Kim Hae-noon, "Students Cite Slip in Respect for Teachers," *Korea JoongAng Daily*, May 14, 2003, http://koreajoongangdaily.joins.com/news/article/article.aspx?aid=1979181.

3. The *kwako* exam originated in the Koryo Dynasty, in the ninth and tenth centuries AD.

4. *Public Spending on Education, Total (% of GDP)*, World Bank, http://data.worldbank.org/indicator/SE.XPD.TOTL.GD.ZS.

5. *The Learning Curve: Lessons in Country Performance in Education*, 2012 Report, Pearson, http://www.into.ie/ROI/NewsEvents/LatestNews/Downloads/LearningCurve.pdf.

6. Kevin Chien-Chang Wu, Ying-Yeh Chen, and Paul S. F. Yip, "Suicide Methods in Asia: Implications in Suicide Prevention," *International Journal of Environmental Research and Public Health*, Mar. 28, 2012, http://www.ncbi.nlm.nih.gov/pmc/articles/PMC3366604/.

7. Jessica Shepherd, "World Education Rankings: Which Country Does Best at Reading, Maths and Science?" *Guardian*,

Dec. 7, 2010, http://www.theguardian.com/news/datablog /2010/dec/07/world-education-rankings-maths-science -reading.

8. Michael Trucano, "Broadband for Schools?" *EduTech*, Feb. 5, 2013, http://blogs.worldbank.org/edutech/broadband.

## 4: CHARACTER IS DESTINY

1. TH Lee, president, GSA Public Relations. The number cited is a largely anecdotal and illustrative character.

2. Official website of Dokdo. The English version can be found at http://en.dokdo.go.kr/korean_dokdo_people_of_dokdo .do.

3. Jack Kim, "North and South Koreans Find Cause for Unity: Japan," Reuters, Nov. 9, 2008, http://www.reuters.com/article /2008/11/19/us-korea-north-japan-idUSTRE4AI12120081119.

4. Lee Moon-yol, "Let's Have North Korea Put a Missile Base on Dokdo," *Dailian*, July 24, 2008, http://www.dailian.co.kr /news/view/119486#reple.

5. The correct literal translation is actually "body and soil are not two," but that doesn't make sense in English.

6. Hyunah Yang, "Vision of Postcolonial Feminist Jurisprudence in Korea: Seen from the 'Family-Head System' in Family Law,"

*Journal of Korean Law* 5(2), 2006: 17–18, http://www.snujkl.org
/?module=file&act=procFileDownload&file_srl=129&sid=fd
d361a9fd3e5565868b15241af3dd20.

## 5: KIMCHI AND THE CABBAGE INFERIORITY COMPLEX

1. "South Korea: SARS Boosts Kimchi Exports to Record Levels," Just-food.com, Jan. 13, 2004, http://www.just-food.com
/news/sars-boosts-kimchi-exports-to-record-levels_id79989
.aspx; "Kimchi Sales Jump Attributed to SARS," *Asia Times/*
Yonhap News Agency, June 19, 2003, http://www.atimes.com
/atimes/Korea/EF19Dg03.html.

2. *Global Status Report on Alcohol and Health: 2011,* World Health
Organization, http://www.who.int/substance_abuse/publications
/global_alcohol_report/msbgsruprofiles.pdf.

3. Millionaires' Club, "The Definitive Ranking of the World's
Million-Case Spirits Brands," Drinks International, 2013, http://
www.drinksint.com/files/CombinednewPDF.pdf.

## 6: WHY POP CULTURE?

1. "Koreans Give Up Their Gold to Help Their Country," *BBC
News,* Jan. 14, 1998, http://news.bbc.co.uk/2/hi/world/analysis
/47496.stm.

2. Geoffrey Cain, "Soap Opera Diplomacy: North Koreans
Crave Banned Videos," *Time,* Oct. 29, 2009., http://content/time
.com/time/word/article/0,8599,1933096,00.html.

## 7: WHEN KOREA BANNED ROCK 'N' ROLL

1. Mark Russell, *Pop Goes Korea* (Berkeley, Cal.: Stone Bridge Press, 2008), excerpted at http://www.markjamesrussell.com/shin-joong-hyun-godfather-of-korean-rock/.

2. This data is from the "official" Ed Sullivan fan site. By Sue's own account, the Kim Sisters appeared on *The Ed Sullivan Show* twenty-two times. See http://www.snujkl.org/?module=file&act=procFileDownload&file_srl=129&sid=fdd361a9fd3e5565868b15241af3dd20.

3. Interview with Nichelle Nichols on NPR, "Star Trek's Uhura Reflects on MLK Encounter," Jan. 17, 2011, http://www.npr.org/2011/01/17/132942461/Star-Treks-Uhura-Reflects-On-MLK-Encounter.

## 8: THE LEAN, MEAN, STAR-MAKING K-POP MACHINE

1. The full contract can be found on the official site of the Korean Central Court; see http://seoul.scourt.go.kr/dcboard/DcNewsViewAction.work?seqnum=6353&gubun=44. English translation of excerpts is available at http://truetvxq.blogspot.com/2010/12/translation-of-contract-profit.html.

2. I asked whether Psy's previous marijuana conviction jeopardized his career. Lee Moon-won said that, as usual, Psy is an exception. "Psy was always a crazy guy; he didn't have a mainstream image."

3. *Report of the International Society of Aesthetic Plastic Surgery*, 2011, http://www.isaps.org/isaps-global-statistics.html.

4. Seoul TouchUp, "Korean Plastic Surgery Clinic: The Plastic Surgery Mecca of the World," http://www.seoultouchup.com /korean-plastic-surgery-clinic-the-plastic-surgery-mecca-of-the -world/. Seoul TouchUp is self-described as "one of the few approved government-approved medical/beauty travel agencies in Korea."

5. Ibid.

## 9: NORTHERN GIRLS, SOUTHERN BOYS

1. "Japan Expels N Korean leader's 'son,'" *BBC News*, May 4, 2001, http://news.bbc.co.uk/2/hi/asia-pacific/1310374.stm.

2. "Ministry of Culture to Expunge 'Peace Studies' Content from Doduk Texts," *Hangyorae*, Jan. 6, 2001, http://www.hani .co.kr/arti/society/schooling/331506.html.

## 10: K-DRAMA: TELEVISION AND THE ORIGINS OF HALLYU

1. It is now referred to simply as American Forces Network.

2. Shim Sungeun, "Behind the Korean Broadcasting Boom," *NHK Broadcasting Studies* 6, 2008: 210–11, http://www.nhk.or .jp/bunken/english/reports/pdf/08_no6_10.pdf.

3. Chu Kun-liang, "Lesson for Taiwan's TV Dramas," *Taiwan Today*, Jan. 15, 2012, http://taiwantoday.tw/ct.asp?xItem=184852 &ctNode=426.

4. Limb Jae-un, "Korean Dramas Find More Fan Bases in Latin America," Korea.net, Mar. 26, 2013, http://www.korea .net/NewsFocus/Culture/view?articleId=106571.

5. Norimitsu Onishi, "What's Korean for 'Real Man'? Ask a Japanese Woman," *New York Times*, Dec. 23, 2004, http://www .nytimes.com/2004/12/23/international/asia/23JAPAN.html ?_r=0.

**11: K-CINEMA: THE JOURNEY FROM CRAP TO CANNES**

1. Further detail on the law can be found in an article by Carolyn Hyun-Kyung Kim, "Building the Korean Film Industry's Competitiveness: Abolish the Screen Quota and Subsidize the Film Industry," *Pacific Rim Law & Policy Journal Association*, 2000. The penalty gets increasingly stringent if the theater does not rectify the failure to meet the quota: "Theaters that violate the screen quota may have their business privileges suspended. If a theater fails to show films for the mandated number of showing days and the violation is for a deficiency of less than twenty days, its business privileges will be suspended one day for every day of the deficiency. If the deficiency exceeds twenty days, the suspension is three days for each day of the deficiency." See http:// digital.law.washington.edu/dspace-law/handle/1773.1/811 ?show=full.

2. "Korean Box Office Top 50," *Letterboxd*, Oct. 6, 2013, http:// letterboxd.com/lifeasfiction/list/korean-box-office-all-time-top -50/. Ranking is in terms of the number of tickets sold.

## 12: HALLYU: THE SHOT HEARD ROUND THE WORLD

1. *Hallyu: From K-Pop to K-Culture* (in Korean). Published jointly by the Ministry of Culture, Sport, and Tourism and the Korean Culture and Information Service, 2012.

2. Chris Kohler, "Q&A: *Mega Man* Creator Wants Japan to Admit Failure," *Wired*, Apr. 12, 2012, http://www.wired.com /gamelife/2012/04/keiji-inafune-qa/.

3. Peter Dyloco, "Can J-Pop Replicate Success of K-Pop?" *Japan Today*, Sept. 15, 2011, http://www.japantoday.com/category /opinions/view/can-j-pop-replicate-success-of-k-pop.

4. "Japan Outranks U.S. in Recorded-Music Sales," *The Japan Times*, Apr. 11, 2013, cited at http://aramatheydidnt.livejournal .com/4776405.html.

5. Helienne Lindvall, "How K-Pop & J-Pop Are Saving Physical Music Sales," *Digital Music News*, Apr. 10, 2013, http:// www.digitalmusicnews.com/permalink/2013/04/10 /kpopjpop.

6. "People Still Buy CDs . . . in Japan. Here's Why," *Bloomberg News*, July 3, 2013, http://www.bloomberg.com/video/pairing-cd-s-with -concert-tickets-boosts-sales-SBWGKQOJSDSdy8T4AkxvNQ .html.

7. *Cahiers du Cinéma* ranked *The Host* one of the top five films released between 2000 and 2009; see http://www.allocine.fr

/article/dossiers/cinema/dossier-18591772/?page=19&
tab=0. *Le Monde* ranked it among the top five films for 2006
on their website published on December 28, 2006; see http://www
.lemonde.fr/cgi-bin/ACHATS/acheter.cgi?offre=ARCHIVES&
type_item=ART_ARCH_30J&objet_id=971215&xtmc=bong
_joon_ho&xtcr=44.

8. Philippe Mesmer, "La Vague Pop Coréenne Gagne l'Europe," *LeMonde*, June 10, 2011, http://www.lemonde.fr/culture
/article/2011/06/09/la-vague-pop-coreenne-gagne-l-europe
_1534023_3246.html.

## 13: KOREA'S SECRET WEAPON: VIDEO GAMES

1. Data provided directly from the the Ministry of Culture,
Sport, and Tourism.

2. Master Blaster, "Japan's 30 Best-Selling Games of All Time,"
Rocketnews24.com, July 8, 2012, http://en.rocketnews24.com
/2012/07/08/japans-best-selling-video-games-of-all-time/.

3. From Aligulac.com, a site devoted to *StarCraft 2* rankings;
current as of November 13, 2013. See http://aligulac.com/.

4. Data from sc2ranks.com, http://www.sc2ranks.com/.

## 14: SAMSUNG: THE COMPANY FORMERLY KNOWN AS SAMSUCK

1. Sea-jin Chang, *Sony vs Samsung: The Inside Story of the Electronics' Giants Battle for Global Supremacy* (Singapore: John Wiley & Sons, 2008).

2. As of November 2013, juries have sided with Apple in a number of cases, and have so far awarded a total of $930 million in damages to Apple. The case is not fully resolved, with Samsung making continued motions and appeals. See "Samsung Owes Apple More than $290 More in Damages, Jury Says," CNET.com, Nov. 21, 2013, http://news.cnet.com/8301-13579_3-57613390-37 /samsung-owes-apple-$290m-more-in-damages-jury-says/.

3. Taken from a report by the analyst group International Data Corporation (IDC); see http://www.idc.com/getdoc.jsp ?containerId=prU.S.23849612.

4. Interbrand's 2012 brand value list can be found at http:// www.interbrand.com/en/best-global-brands/previous-years /2012/Best-Global-Brands-2012-Brand-View.aspx.

5. "Look Out, Sony!" *Forbes*, Apr. 16, 2001, http://www.forbes .com/global/2001/0416/028.html.

6. Frank Rose, "Seoul Machine," *Wired*, May 2005, http:// www.wired.com/wired/archive/13.05/samsung.html.

7. Peter Lewis, "A Perpetual Crisis Machine," *Fortune*, Sept. 19, 2005, cited at http://www.fortunechina.com/first/content/2008 -02/22/content_4879.htm.

8. Ibid.

9. Ibid.

## 15: THE MINISTRY OF FUTURE CREATION

1. Kim Tae-jong, "Ministry of ICT: Give Pay Cut to Who Named It!" *Korea Times*, Apr. 3, 2013, http://www.koreatimes.co.kr/www/news/biz/2013/04/123_133293.html.

2. "South Korea's Ten Largest Chaebols Represent 80 Percent of Korean GDP," *East Economist*, Jan. 6, 2013, http://www.easteconomist.com/2013/01/south-koreas-ten-largest-chaebols-create-80-of-korean-gdp/.

3. Jeong Kim, "A Return to South Korea, Thwarted by Nationalism," *The Washington Post*, March 29, 2013, http://www.washingtonpost.com/opinions/jeong-kim-a-return-to-south-korea-thwarted-by-nationalism/2013/03/29/fa674336-97f8-11e2-814b-063623d80a60_story.html.

4. Ryu Kyong-dong, "Future Ministry Officials Waiting to Be Assigned Have No Future," *Korea IT News*, May 7, 2013, http://english.itnews.com/policy/2762896_1302.html.

5. Max Chafkin, "The Returnees," *Inc.*, Dec. 2011, http://www.inc.com/magazine/201112/the-returnees.html.

6. Ibid.

7. Ibid.

# ACKNOWLEDGMENTS

· · · · · · · · · · · · · · · · · · · · · · ·

My agents and editors, who saw a book where there was none: George Lucas at Inkwell, Lizzy Kremer at David Higham, Anna deVries and Stephen Morrison at Picador, Abigail Bergstrom and Briony Gowlett at Simon & Schuster UK. Where would I be without them? Nothing and nowhere. They showed remarkable restraint even though it was clear I had no idea what I was doing. Anna of the incisive pen and diplomatic tongue deserves special mention. She could have written ten books with the time she devoted to editing mine. Oh Captain, my Captain.

My Korean ground team, who donated countless hours of their time to help me with this book, and who were selfless and generous beyond all reckoning. TH Lee and Minhee Sohn at GSA Public Relations: you are the most capable people I have ever met or ever shall meet. A special, heartfelt thanks to Daniel Gray of O'ngo Food Communications and Charm Lee at the Korean Tourism Organization. I was greatly inspired by author Kyung-sook Shin and the great minds behind Paju Book City. Thank you, Bobby Kwak and Khee Lee, for your kind assistance.

Longtime mentor Peter Beinart and his gracious and graceful wife, Diana, who have always welcomed me as a fellow rootless cosmopolitan. The magnificent couple Elisha and Lynn Wiesel, for their good humor, good nature, impeccable hosting abilities, and for their almost preternatural generosity and understanding. Elie and Marion Wiesel, who were very influential on my world view, literary sensibilities, and ethical education—sorry about the dry cleaning bill. Susan and Joseph Ditkoff, who have witnessed all my life stages with bemusement, but who have always reserved judgment. The brilliant, compassionate Rana Choi, a fellow "son of Ben," whatever we meant by that. High school friend Yonhee Cha. Yale chums Stephen and Helen Lee. Helen Fessenden—you are intelligent, kind, and a godsend. Charles Ardai, a writer with too many talents and boundless creative advice. Robert Thomson, who gave me my first big break at the *Financial Times*. Jonathan Zittrain at Harvard Law School, for being plain terrific. Damien McGuinness—my Berlin cohort—who read the first short story I ever wrote and encouraged me to turn it into what became my first book. Midnight Madness Game Control, for letting me make final edits on my manuscript when I was supposed to be barring people from approaching the hint givers.

S. Mitra Kalita for her inspiring creativity and work ethic, and for forcing me to write that article about growing up in Gangnam.

This is the "I stand on the shoulders of giants" bit: were it not for the likes of Chang-rae Lee, Jeannie Park, Amy Tan, and Jeff Yang making strides for Asian-American writers, there would be no apparatus for a book like this to exist.

My Paris friends. First, the writers from the La Rotonde luncheons, for welcoming me into your esteemed company and for reminding me why I became a writer: Diane Johnson, Jake Lamar, Barbara Chase Riboud, Mavis Gallant, Ward Just, William J. Smith. Dinny, you are an inspiration as an artist, hostess, scholar, and human being. I am blessed to know you.

My dear, dear France 24 mates Khatya "Gravitas" Chhor, James "l'Ombre" Creedon, Leela "Swinger" Jacinto, Katherine "You Can't Polish a Turd" Thompson, Tony "Solomon the Wise" Todd. Vaila Finch: I am touched by your unswerving affection and friendship. Charlotte Wilkins: Lizzy to my Jane, your literary stardom is all but inevitable. Derek Thomson and Raina Lampkins-Fielder, who survived the journey from exasperated boss to invaluable friends. Jarvis Cocker, for teaching me the "Five Years On" rule, to which I still adhere. Helen Cho, a brilliant second set of eyes for this manuscript, fellow French slumlord, and another writer to watch.

To the city of Paris: *Comme a écrit Hugo: "Si l'on demandait à l'énorme ville: Qu'est-ce que c'est que cela? elle répondrait: C'est mon petit."*

And my supportive and adoring and much adored family, who have put up with a lot of petulant behavior from me this year. Always, for that matter.